GREAT CHRISTIAN THINKERS

John of the Cross

DEMCO

Praise for Other Titles in the Great Christian Thinkers Series

AUGUSTINE Richard Price
'... admirably clear, concise, and though sometimes critical, written with great sympathy and understanding of Augustine's problems, and of the historical context within which he was labouring.' MICHAEL WALSH, *BUTLER'S LIVES OF THE SAINTS* AND *BOOK OF SAINTS*

FRANCIS & BONAVENTURE Paul Rout
'This book meets a real need ... a painless way into Bonaventure's life and thinking, both as a philosopher, a man of prayer and as a great Franciscan.' SISTER FRANCES TERESA, OSC, THE COMMUNITY OF THE POOR CLARES, ARUNDEL

JOHN OF THE CROSS Wilfrid McGreal
'We are greatly indebted to Fr Wilfrid McGreal for bringing alive in such an accessible way the mysticism and mystery of St John of the Cross.' GEORGE CAREY, ARCHBISHOP OF CANTERBURY

THOMAS MORE Anne Murphy
'This superb piece of scholarship sheds new light on the enduring importance of the unity between Thomas More's life and thought. Anne Murphy shows how this large-hearted Christian was a great European and an outstanding example of personal and public integrity.' GERALD O'COLLINS, GREGORIAN UNIVERSITY, ROME

KIERKEGAARD Peter Vardy
'This is a fascinating introduction to Kierkegaard's prophetic insights into the nature of Christian faith, insights which we desperately need to ponder today.' GERALD HUGHES, AUTHOR OF *GOD OF SURPRISES*

SIMONE WEIL Stephen Plant
'Stephen Plant portrays the immense strength and the touching vulnerability of Simone Weil, the complex nature of her convictions, and the startling and continuing relevance of her views today.' DONALD ENGLISH, CHAIRMAN OF THE WORLD METHODIST COUNCIL

JOHN OF THE CROSS

Wilfrid McGreal, O Carm

SERIES EDITOR: PETER VARDY

Triumph
Liguori, Missouri

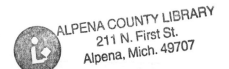

Published by Triumph
An Imprint of Liguori Publications
Liguori, Missouri

Library of Congress Cataloging-in-Publication Data

McGreal, Wilfrid.
    John of the Cross / Wilfrid McGreal. — 1st U.S. ed.
       p.   cm. (Great Christian thinkers)
    Includes bibliographical references and index.
    ISBN 0-7648-0114-7
    1. John of the Cross, Saint, 1542–1591. I. Title. II. Series.
BX4700.J7M37   1997
271'.7302—dc21
[B]   96-52494

Originally published in English by HarperCollinsPublishers Ltd under the title:
John of the Cross by Wilfrid McGreal

First U.S. Edition 1997
01 00 99 98 97   5 4 3 2 1
Printed in the United States of America

Contents

Acknowledgement

I would like to offer my thanks to Ros Duddell, who did much to enable this book to reach its final form.

Date Chart

John's life	General Events
	1492 Conquest of Granada – Moors expelled from Spain Columbus discovers America
	1517 Martin Luther posts his theses at Wittenberg
	1527 Sack of Rome by Emperor Charles V
	1534 Founding of the Jesuits Act of Supremacy establishes Church of England
1540 John (de Yepes) born at Fontiveros	
1545 Don Gonzalo his father dies	1545–63 Council of Trent reforms Roman Catholic Church
1551 Family move to Medina del Campo	
	1556–98 Philip II King of Spain
	1558–1603 Queen Elizabeth I

1562   St Teresa establishes the
       Reform at St Joseph's, Avila
1563   John enters the Carmelites
       at Medina
1567   John ordained at
       Salamanca
1568   John part of first
       community of Reformed
       friars at Duruelo

                                          1571   Don Juan defeats Turks at
                                                 Battle of Lepanto

1572–77 John confessor at the
       Monastery of the
       Incarnation at Avila
1577   Dec. – John imprisoned at
       the Priory at Toledo
1578   Aug. – Escapes from Toledo
1580   His mother Doña Catalina
       dies
1582–6 Prior at Granada where
       he writes most of his
       poems and commentaries
1588   Prior of Segovia and
       assistant to Nicolas Doria,
       the new head of the
       Reform

                                          1588   Destruction of the
                                                 Armada

1591   June – John destined to go
       to Mexico – loses all offices
       Sept. – Moves to Ubeda –
       already ill
       14 Dec. – Dies at Ubeda

Date Chart

		1541–1613 El Greco
		1547–1616 Cervantes
		1564–1616 Shakespeare
1618	First edition of John's works	
1630	First complete edition of his writings	
1726	Benedict XIII canonizes him	
1952	Named patron of Spanish poets	

Introduction

This is a book about a man with a sublime imagination. He was the victim of misunderstanding by those who should have appreciated him. Faced with darkness and cruel treatment, he responded with great poetry that sings of the highest experience of love. The man is Juan de Yepes (1540–1591), known as John of the Cross. He came from Castile in the heart of Spain and lived most of his life as a member of a community of brothers or friars, the Carmelites.

John has a message and a vision of life that can have real meaning for people today. His poems, born in darkness and personal tragedy, even with a sense of the loss of God, find God in the midst of sorrows. For John, the healing presence of God could be found in dark, unlikely places. He also believed that our human longings, our deepest desires can only find fulfilment in God. John claimed to have found that closeness and fulfilment and wanted to share his experience and the possibility of that experience with others. The way to this intimacy with God is a way of letting go of what could seem dearest and most important in life. John's teaching is challenging but it is not abstract, it is not unreal. It comes from the heart and speaks the language of the imagination.

As John of the Cross, the man, is probably scarcely known in the English-speaking world, this introduction provides a biographical sketch. The section on John as a poet and mystic is meant to give a flavour of his poetic genius. John's poems spring directly from the moments in his life when he believed he was intimate with God. The rest of the book attempts to pick out the key themes and concerns which run through his other writings.

Can John say anything to people today? In his own day, John was concerned to be a genuine guide to people searching for personal growth and help in their quest for God. In an age when many guides and gurus prove to be bogus, does John offer a wisdom that transcends time? John was a passionate, caring person who wanted only the best for those he guided. This book will hopefully enable his voice to be heard by men and women at the end of the twentieth century.

John's Life and Background

The sixteenth century was an age of upheaval, discovery and change. It was the century of the Reformation and the time when Europeans ventured out to the Americas and the Indies. It was also the century of the Renaissance, an age of creativity in the arts and sciences. In England, figures such as Shakespeare, Drake and Elizabeth I stand out. In Spain, Philip II is a dominant political figure while John of the Cross is the great poet of the age and also an outstanding teacher for Christians searching for God.

John of the Cross deserves to be better known in the English-speaking world. He has a message for our age and he needs to be given a hearing. Up to now, John has not been well served by his biographers, most of whom have presented him as a remote, rather severe saint. John's humanity has been removed and religious clichés and miracles have obscured the real person.

To understand John's life and what he stands for means finding out something about sixteenth-century Spain. Spain was at the height of its power during John's lifetime. But it was also a new country, something like the United States is even today. Most of modern Spain was conquered by Islamic invaders from North Africa in the eighth century. It took six hundred years to drive the invaders out and it was only at the end of the fifteenth century that the south of Spain was reconquered.

The end of Moorish rule coincided with the discovery of the Americas and the establishment of an empire in Mexico and South America. Wealth flowed into Spain and the country flourished.

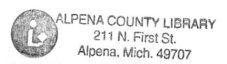

However, Spain was still a mixture of peoples. Germanic and Celtic people lived alongside Jews and folk with North African origins. There was also a religious mix – Christian, Jewish and Muslim. The official policy of the government was to expel Jews and Muslims or to force them to become Christians if they wanted to remain in Spain. There were, therefore, tensions among the different racial groups, and the Inquisition, which was very much an arm of the State, worked to achieve stability.

The Spanish Inquisition had originally been an organ of the Catholic Church, but from the sixteenth century onwards, orthodoxy, uniformity and national unity became part of an overall process. Philip II wanted to control the Church so that it served the interests of Spain first and foremost. This control and the fear aroused by the Inquisition was to cast a shadow over the life of John of the Cross.

Childhood

According to the latest research, John de Yepes, to give him his family name, was born in 1540 at Fontiveros in Castile, in the very heart of Spain. John did not have an easy childhood; he knew poverty and insecurity. His parents came from opposite sides of the social divide. His father, Gonzalo de Yepes, came from a prosperous business family who lived in Toledo. They were merchants dealing in textiles and enjoyed a comfortable life given the expanding economy. However, they had their insecurities as they were *Conversos*, Jewish converts to Christianity.

They had been Catholics for some generations, but there was always the fear that a business rival could rake up the information to do them down. The omnipresent Inquisition, which operated like a secret service, posed a threat. It was easy enough to be denounced by the Inquisition and end up penniless.

It was in the course of buying cloth that Gonzalo met his future wife, Catalina Alvarez. She was a weaver, living and working in

Fontiveros, near Madrid. Gonzalo's family were against the marriage, ostensibly because of the social gulf, but historians argue that there was another motive. It is claimed that Catalina lacked *limpieza de sangre* – purity of blood. She was, it is believed, of Moorish origin – a descendant of the Muslim invaders. Gonzalo's family were frightened and felt that such a marriage could put the spotlight on them and people would then discover their Jewish origins.

Gonzalo was unwilling to give up Catalina so they married, even though he was disowned by his family and the couple started out in life penniless. Gonzalo learned the skill of weaving from his wife and together they struggled to earn enough money to keep a roof over their heads.

John was the youngest of three boys born to this tenacious couple, but tragically, when John was five years old, his father died, a victim of the plague which was the scourge of the poor at that time. Gonzalo's family were unwilling to help Catalina and her three young sons, so she struggled as best she could to bring up the boys on her own. She moved north to Medina Del Campo, a busy market town, where she found a more secure outlet for her weaving. However, tragedy struck again when Luis, the middle son, died. John by now was eight years old.

Gifted and Caring

The plight of single parents then as now was hard. John was growing up on the wrong side of the tracks, and yet marvellous bonds of love and loyalty grew up between the boys and their mother. John was able to get some basic education at a school for the poor, the Colegio de la Doctrine. Medina was a vibrant, exciting place, and John loved to hear stories of the Americas and enjoyed the bustle of the market. He must have seemed a waif, he was so small – as an adult he was barely five feet tall. He was also dark-skinned, more African than European in looks.

When John was twelve, he was asked to work in a local hospital. The hospital administrator, Don Alonso, was to prove a generous friend. Las Bubas, as the hospital was called, housed patients with contagious diseases. John was asked to be a nursing assistant and so for the next six years or so he cared for the sick, feeding them, washing them and dressing their sores. This was a period when syphilis was rampant, so many of the patients were dying slow, painful deaths, shunned by family and locked often in deep anger and denial. The young John gave of his energy to care for those abandoned by society. He spent hours chatting, telling stories and singing the songs he had learned in the market-place. In addition to this caring, John helped raise funds and collected food for the hospital.

Don Alonso recognized that John was a gifted young man and paid for him to study at the newly established Jesuit College in Medina – perhaps John might become a priest and care for the sick. For the next three years, John studied literature, the classics and philosophy, enjoying the challenge of study and especially the chance to write. Here he had his literary formation, the future poet learning his craft.

The Carmelites

John still helped out at the hospital and it seemed natural that John should get ordained and become the hospital chaplain. John wanted to give his life to God but he felt that if he was going to be a priest he would like to belong to a community, a family. So, in 1563, he decided to join the community of Carmelite friars at the Priory of Santa Ana in Medina. Why did he join that community, and who were these Carmelite friars?

As to the why of his joining the Carmelite Community, the answer is probably quite simple. Pablo Garrido, who has specialized in the history of the period, believes that some of John's father's family had been members of the Carmelite Order at

Toledo. He cites Diego de Yepes and an Andres de Yepes, who were members of the Carmelite Community in Toledo in the early years of the sixteenth century. They could have been his forebears and perhaps were an unconscious influence.

The Carmelites were part of a movement in the development of Christianity which occurred in the early thirteenth century. The Church of the day seemed out of touch with the people, and the simplicity of the gospel seemed to have been lost. In this context, groups of Christians seeking to live a simple life based on the gospel emerged in Europe. One such group, centred on St Francis of Assisi, was the origin of the Franciscans, an order of brothers or friars who lived and preached the poverty of Christ. The Carmelites did not have a leader or founder, but the order grew out of a group of pilgrims who had settled on Mount Carmel. These pilgrims, who had journeyed to the Holy Land seeking a closer union with Christ, began to live as a community on Mount Carmel and were given a rule of life in 1208 by the Patriarch of Jerusalem. Like the Franciscans, the Carmelites lived as a group of brothers committed to prayer but also ready to go out and preach to the Christian groups in the Holy Land.

These men chose Mount Carmel as their home because it had links with the great prophet Elijah, and its beauty caused it to be seen as a symbol of God's grace. It was because the Order originated on Mount Carmel that its members became known as Carmelites.

The first Carmelites lived out their contemplative lifestyle in the Holy Land for some fifty years. They lived according to their rule, meditating day and night on the Word of the Lord'. The praying of the Scriptures and daily eucharist were at the heart of the life of these early Carmelites. They constructed little cells around the spring of Elijah and, because of their commitment, many pilgrims and Crusaders were drawn to what must have seemed an idyllic way of life.

However, the politics of the day broke in on this peaceful community. The Crusaders were forced out of the Holy Land and groups of Carmelites came to the West, refugees from violence. Once in Western Europe, the Order, which had received Papal approval in 1247, had to decide how they should live. At a meeting held at Aylesford in Kent in 1247, delegates representing the groups who had come from the Holy Land decided that their way of life should be one of serving the people by preaching the Gospel. The Carmelites decided, like the Franciscans, to go out among the people preaching in the market-places or opening churches in the new towns. They would depend for their livelihood on the people's generosity, they would be preaching brothers who begged for their living. The official Church was to call these groups – Carmelites, Franciscans and Dominicans – mendicant friars.

The Carmelites had their own distinctive vision which came from their origins in the Holy Land. When they came to Europe and became involved in active ministry in the growing urban centres, they brought with them memories and symbols. Mount Carmel, with its beauty and solitude, was a symbol of God's goodness but also a challenge. The challenge was to retain a sense of solitude and stillness so that even in the busiest of places there would be a space for God. Again, because Mount Carmel was associated with the great prophet Elijah, who was outspoken and yet close to God in prayer, the Carmelites have always tried to incorporate his spirit into their lifestyle. Finally, like all Christians in the Middle Ages, the Carmelites had great devotion to Mary the mother of Jesus. They admired her trust, her faith and they saw her as a model of discipleship.

The medieval Carmelites and their successors have tried to create a synthesis whereby they could be involved in the outreach of the Church but at the same time they have tried to keep alive a sense of reflective scriptural prayer and silence. The attempts to create a way of life which is rooted in silence and prayer and yet involves working in society as preachers, teachers and answering people's deepest needs have always created tensions.

It was this order of brothers, with its traditions rooted in the

Holy Land, that John joined in 1563 at Medina del Campo. The Carmelite friars in Castile were not numerous but were known for their faithfulness in keeping their rule. The Middle Ages had seen many communities of monks, nuns or friars become quite mediocre, but the Carmelites of Castile were a fervent group.

John was one of a group of young Carmelites studying and learning the traditions of the Order. Since the Carmelites, like other friars, were preachers, they needed a good formation. People looked to the friars to provide them with sound doctrine as so often in the Middle Ages the parish clergy were poorly educated. John and his contemporaries spent their year of initiation or noviciate learning about the Order's traditions and being helped to grow in their relationship with God. They would also have had classes in literature and philosophy, learning how to formulate and express ideas and also being given a sound cultural basis. From contemporary documentation it seems that John's fellow students were a lively and committed group. After a year of initiation, John and his companions moved to Salamanca to study theology. Salamanca was highly regarded as an academic centre on a par with Paris or Oxford. John's studies would have covered the Scriptures and he would have been introduced to great figures of Christian thought such as St Augustine and St Thomas Aquinas. His lectures would have been in Latin and the style of teaching, called scholasticism, was rooted in Greek philosophy. It might seem rather foreign to us, but it was intellectually challenging and gave John a means of expressing his ideas.

While John studied at Salamanca he also had a chance to read books written by Carmelites from the early years of the Order. These writers were to give John a thirst for journeying closer to God. *The Fiery Arrow*, written in 1270, not long after the Carmelites came to Europe, was the work of a French Carmelite who wanted his brothers to preserve the ideals of the Order's earliest days and not be swamped by over-activity. He also stressed the need for sound formation and intellectual vigour. Another book,

The Institutions of the First Monks, written by a Catalan Carmelite, Philip Ribot, stresses the role of reflective prayer and challenges his colleagues to aspire to close union with God – nothing less should be the goal.

The Influence of Teresa of Avila

In 1567, John was ordained as a priest in the Carmelite Order. It was at this stage that he met a remarkable woman who was to have as deep an influence on his life as his mother. The woman was Teresa de Alumada y Cepeda, better known as Teresa of Avila. Teresa was a Carmelite nun. The Carmelites, like most orders in the Church, had set up a way of life for women so they could live the spirit and inspiration of the Order. Teresa was a remarkable woman with a vision. She wanted to bring the Carmelite Order closer in spirit and practice to its earliest days in the Holy Land. She wanted communities where prayer and silence were high on the agenda. What she was calling for was a Reform or Renewal of life in the Order for both friars and nuns. The Prior General, the head of the Order, John Rossi, had given her permission to found convents where this more fervent living of the Carmelite ideal could be fostered. Teresa had won the heart of John Rossi, who commented that she was worth a hundred friars.

When John met Teresa she was already fifty, twice his age. She came from a well-to-do family, and as a girl had shown independence and a romantic nature. For many years she had lived an unremarkable life in her convent at Avila, but around the age of forty she had profound religious experiences which had a radical effect on her and gave her the energy to begin her work of renewal among the Carmelites. Teresa was also the author of books chronicling her experiences, her *Life* and *The Way of Perfection*. Teresa was impressed by John and saw that he would be a likely candidate to help her with her work. At this time, John was going through a spell of being shy and wanting to withdraw from the rush of life. Teresa persuaded him to go back to finish his studies at Salamanca but to keep an open mind about working for her project. Teresa's comment on John at this time makes play about his height: 'Though he is small in stature he is great in God's eyes'.

When John had finished his studies in 1568, Teresa approached the superior of the Carmelite friars in Castile, Alonzo Gonzalez, and asked him to allow some of his friars to live according to her renewed vision or Reform. In the first instance, she wanted friars who would help her nuns by hearing confessions and giving them guidance. John was willing to join in the project, as was Antonio de Heredia, who had been in charge of forming new members of the Order. However, Teresa wanted to make it clear that her Reform was not meant to be superficial – something measured by austerity and ascetic practices. She wanted a way of living with balance so that charity, detachment and humility mattered more than doing spectacular penances. Teresa was interested in creating environments where genuine humanity could flourish. She was to show John that what was vital was the development of the creative and the imaginative in the life of a Christian. She helped him see that academic life had overshadowed the playful, creative side of his nature. His love of music, of poetry, story-telling – these were rediscovered and became central in his development. As John was to grow as a great teacher, it was his creative gifts that enabled him to communicate his profound experiences.

The Reform

A new way of life began for John on 28 November 1568 at Duruelo, a small village between Avila and Salamanca. On that day, he, Antonio and Joseph celebrated mass, presided over by the head of the Carmelite Order in Castile, Alonzo Gonzalez. The three friars put on habits made of coarse cloth and promised to live by a vision of Carmelite life that would reflect its early years on Mount Carmel. They wanted to turn their backs on any mitigation of the original Rule of the Order. To mark this moment as decisive, John took a new name and was to be known as John of the Cross. This way of life eventually gained the title of Discalced Reform – the term Discalced means 'barefoot'. Being barefoot was a sign of reform in religious communities in the sixteenth century, although in the case of these Carmelites it meant wearing rough sandals.

The first priory of what was to be called the Reform was an old barn that the friars were to turn into a simple dwelling. John was delighted at the development. Living this simple prayerful life fulfilled his heart's desire. There was another reason for John to be happy as his mother volunteered to act as cook while his brother, Francisco, came over to help in the restoration of the building. John never lost close links with his family, loving to spend time with them.

The new way of life or Reform began to spread with new priories being founded. John was soon called to leave Duruelo to help care for the young friars who were studying for ordination at Alcalá, near Madrid. This was a role which John relished, as he had come to realize that the whole person had to be developed. Academic attainment was essential but these young men needed to value the traditions of the Order and be well-grounded in humanity if they were to help people.

Not everyone in this new movement among the Carmelites had the same balanced view of life. The new entrants or novices to the Order at nearby Pastrana found themselves under a novice master who had gone overboard with asceticism. In the name of the quest for holiness, the Novice Master had introduced bizarre and irrational practices. The spectacular had taken the place of the spiritual. John, mindful of Teresa's advice, was able to see the lack of balance. He realized the young men needed proper food and adequate sleep and reintroduced laughter into their lives. John knew that what really mattered was an inner conversion, and he believed God wanted a loving, generous person.

In 1572, John was given what proved to be a daunting task. He was asked to go to Avila to be confessor to the Convent of the Incarnation. This was the convent where Teresa of Avila began her life as a nun. It was a huge community of 130 nuns beset by poverty and full of factions. In 1571, despite the protests of the community, Teresa had been made Prioress, and Angel de Salazar, who was now in charge of the Order in Castile, gave her his full support. By January 1573, the convent was at peace and open to creative change. While much of the credit must go to Teresa, she could not have set so much change in motion without John's help. John lived in a small house near the convent and was to stay there until 1577. John gave of himself generously and won the confidence of the community. He was deeply sensitive in dealing with the nuns, recognizing each person's uniqueness. A typical piece of generosity was the famous drawing of the Crucified Christ which he made for one of the nuns, Ana Mary of Jesus. Centuries later, the drawing was to inspire Salvador Dali's masterpiece, *Saint John of the Cross*.

These five years at Avila were a time of mutual enrichment for John and Teresa. By this time, Teresa was deeply advanced in the mystical life – she lived sensing God's closeness to her. She shared many of her insights and experiences with John, helping him in turn make sense of the profound things happening in his life. Their friendship was a precious gift and perhaps can teach us today to value friendship and such creative intimacy. John and Teresa were obviously attracted to each other but in a way that respected the other's role and journey in life.

During this period in Avila, John continued to make time for the poor and disadvantaged. He was always ready to preach and spend time listening to people, especially the sick. He also remembered his own impoverished childhood and found time to teach poor children the basics of reading and writing. And, as ever, he found time for his mother and brother.

Punishment and Imprisonment

In 1577, John's life was turned upside down by events outside of his control. The Reform or Renewal of the Order which John had helped initiate was now the subject of controversy and suspicion. Originally, the leadership of the Order had supported the Reform, but they had imposed certain restrictions. One such restriction was to limit the number of priories committed to the new way, and also not to set up communities of the Reform in Andalusia. The reason behind these restrictions was the experience of similar reforms in Italy developing too quickly and being taken over by the immature and enthusiasts. These restrictions were now being ignored, chiefly because King Philip II began to interfere in the internal affairs of the Order. Philip had an obsession with Church affairs and wanted to exercise as much control over the Spanish Church as possible, resenting the influence of the Pope and any order coming from Rome. As a result of this interference, a whole tangle of misunderstanding developed among the Carmelites. Those friars who had not joined the Reform felt threatened by the growth of the new foundations, and the head of the Order in Rome, John Rossi, felt slighted. Communications between Spain and Rome were painfully slow, and letters which could have clarified matters arrived too late.

The perception grew both in Rome and among those in charge of the Order in Spain that the movement inspired originally to renew the Carmelite way of life was getting out of hand, and that certain personalities were becoming far too independent. It was in this context that John was seen as a leader of what was now viewed as a disobedient group. John became the focus of criticism because he had been among the first to commit himself to the movement which was now called the Reform.

In December 1577, John was forcibly taken by a group of friars from Avila to the Carmelite Priory at Toledo. Here, John was accused by the superiors of the Carmelite Order in Castile of being rebellious and disobedient. He was subjected to the punishments laid down in the Statutes of the Order of that time. These included solitary confinement and being flogged. Some biographers describe his imprisonment at Toledo in great detail, although such accounts are fiction, as we have few details about the eight months of John's imprisonment. However, the whole period must have been a time of terrible trauma. John must have wondered why he was the focus of such anger, why should people who were supposed to be idealistic act in such a harsh way? John's imprisonment and abduction seem very like the fate of modern-day hostages. What we do know is that during this tragic, cruel time John had profound religious experiences which he was able to express in sublime poetry. The long months of imprisonment brought him close to God and saw an awakening of a great artistic gift.

John managed to escape from his prison in the high summer of 1578. His captors grew careless, and in the middle of the night he managed to slip out of the priory. Nuns at a nearby convent gave him shelter, and with the help of friends, John found his way to a priory belonging to the Reform.

The tensions in the Carmelite Order diminished as misunderstandings were ironed out and the priories belonging to the Reform began to have their own organization and became more or less independent from those not wanting to embrace it. The Reform began to be called Discalced, or 'barefoot', while the rest were known as Observants.

Given this happier climate, John was able to get on with his life. He soon recovered from his imprisonment and was asked to help in a newly-founded Priory in Andalusia. John was to spend the next ten years of his life in the South of Spain. It was a totally different landscape to his native Castile, but John fell in love with the rugged countryside. Nature was to be an important part of his life from now on. He loved walking and would often walk up to fifty miles to see a friend. He liked nothing better than the feel of the wind and the sun, and his brother Francisco tells how the night sky fascinated him. He would often spend hours staring at the beauty of the stars.

During these ten years, John's life was rich and varied. He held many responsible posts in the administration of the Order. He taught many of the young friars and gave numerous lectures to the Carmelite nuns. This was the time when he wrote his poetry and composed his commentaries on the poems. From 1582 to 1588, John was Prior of the newly-founded Carmelite Priory in Granada. The Priory, called Los Martires, was built on the hill of the Alhambra. The Alhambra was a complex of Moorish palaces and fortifications, and even today it strikes visitors as one of the wonders of the world. John admired the delicate Moorish architecture and the beautiful flowers that covered the surrounding hills. Gardens, design and engineering were all important in John's life. He delighted in designing gardens for any newly founded priory or convent. When building was in progress, John loved to choose the stone and work along with the architect so that the building would be a home, not an institution. One of his great achievements was to design the aqueduct that brought water from the Alhambra to the Priory in Granada.

The only cloud in John's life during this time was his mother's death. He had loved her dearly and knew how she had struggled to give him and his brother the best possible home. John found time in these years to help many of the friars and nuns, guiding them in their search for God. He also proved a loving friend to a whole host of people. By the end of his years in Granada, John was at the height of his powers but also had flowered as a most loving and lovable man. Small, dark, intense, but also humorous, gifted and loyal.

Rebellious

The last years of John's life, between 1588 and 1591, saw the clouds returning again. The leadership of the Discalced Reform had passed to Nicholás Doria. Doria was a great administrator (he had been a banker before joining the Carmelites), but a man who loved discipline and abhorred laxity. Doria clashed with Jerome Gracián, a charismatic figure, a friend of Teresa of Avila and Doria's predecessor as head of the Reform. Gracián had been the dynamo at the heart of the Reform, responsible for its expansion. It had been Gracián's impetuosity in the 1570s which had created the situation that led to John's imprisonment.

Doria now wanted to contain Gracián, and the rift between the two came to a head when Doria expelled Gracián from the Discalced Reform. John, by this time, was back in the Castile Priory at Segovia and was Doria's deputy in the running of the Order. John saw the rift between Doria and Gracián as power politics and made it clear that this was no way to behave. Doria, a cold personality, saw John's attitude as rebellious and became very negative towards him.

A whispering campaign began against John, orchestrated by Diego Evangelista, one of Doria's lieutenants. Diego disliked John because in years gone by John had had to discipline him. The word went out that John's writings were heretical and that his behaviour was suspect. A posting to Mexico was mooted, but instead ill-health intervened. In 1591, John was sent to a remote priory in Andalusia where he settled down to live a simple life of prayer and to work on the farm attached to the Priory. Meanwhile, the whispering campaign continued, with hints that John's teaching on prayer was not in keeping with orthodox teaching.

Diego claimed that John was teaching people to be independent of the Church in their prayer lives. This was a period when any departure or seeming departure from orthodoxy was viewed with grave concern. The Reformation had fragmented Christianity so the need to preserve an embattled Church was paramount. Sadly, Doria did nothing to counter the rumours and this did little to help John's frail health. By the autumn of 1591, John was seriously ill. The indications are that John probably had some form of skin cancer which eventually became localized as a tumour on the spine.

John was transferred to the Priory at Ubeda where it was hoped he could receive some medical treatment. However, John's troubles were compounded as the Prior of the Community resented the presence of an invalid. He saw John merely as a financial burden. Eventually, John managed to penetrate the Prior's hostility and the resentment vanished. John died on 14 December 1591. On his deathbed, he asked the community to read from the Song of Songs, which was his favourite scriptural text. He found comfort in the words expressing sublime love, and his final words were ones of trust: 'Into your hands, Lord, I commend my spirit.' In his dying he found a peace that had often been elusive during his life.

John of the Cross emerges as a man who grew in humanity as he searched for holiness. His life as a Carmelite was not always easy but he came out of the trauma of his imprisonment without bitterness and turned the negative experience into a source of creativity. His last months were overshadowed by the whispering campaign and sheer insensitivity, but again he was able to rise above the pettiness. John had a strength and resilience that is really admirable. He was never one to show resentment but got on with the business of living. He did not allow other people to set the agenda for his life. His strength was his ability to rise above rivalries. What does emerge is a sense that he had a wonderfully warm personality and he really had a great love for people. He always valued his family, especially his mother, and after her death he found great comfort in his closeness to his brother Francisco and Francisco's wife. John, while he was a great poet and a wonderful teacher, always remained very domestic. He loved caring for people and when he had roles of responsibility, he used the position to make priories and convents happier places. He enjoyed organizing picnics on feast days, and, as has been noted, his practical talents included designing gardens and solving engineering problems. However, besides all this energy and giftedness, there was a basic grit and determination in the man. His early years, his awareness of poverty gave him a sense of realism and helped him survive persecution and hardship. John, though, was not remote or forbidding; he was gifted, lovable and single-minded in his love of God.

Doria died shortly after John and the whispering campaign petered out. Gradually, John's works were published and his teaching was recognized for its beauty and profundity. Official recognition came when the Church declared him a saint in 1726, while the literary world gave its accolade when he was named patron of Spanish poets in 1952.

2

Poet and Mystic

When John was imprisoned by his fellow Carmelites he underwent profound religious experiences. In the middle of physical suffering he had what he believed was an amazing experience of closeness to God, so close as to be akin to a physical union. John wanted to share this experience, and the result is his poetry which is among the finest in the Spanish language. It reads as powerfully today as when it was first composed.

John's deep sense of union with the divine is often called 'mystical'. All the great religions of the world acknowledge the reality of mystical experience. In fact, today many scholars find the mystical an important bond between the great faiths. One such scholar is William Johnston, a Catholic who lives and works in Japan and has a special interest in Buddhism. He also sees John of the Cross as a mystic who has an important message for people today.

In the modern world, while many people would have little to do with organized religion, there is still a deep thirst for meaning in life, for a relationship which could satisfy our deepest longings. Can John of the Cross help such people, and can we find a language that will speak to people from different backgrounds as they search for meaning?

If we go to John of the Cross we will find words like 'love', 'knowledge' and 'secret' having a great importance. John speaks of a secret knowledge that comes through love: love is at the heart of such knowledge and it is a gift. In the Christian tradition, the relationship between the individual and God is always seen as being initiated by God. It is God who loves us first and we gradually become aware of God wanting to be part of our lives. St Paul and St John the Evangelist both emphasize the primacy of God's love for us. St Paul writes to the first Christians at Ephesus: '... he chose us in Christ before the foundation of the world to be holy and blameless before him in love' (EPHESIANS 1:4). St John, in his First Letter, writes:

> In this is love, not that we loved God but that he loved us and sent his Son to be the atoning sacrifice for our sins ...
>
> God is love, and those who abide in love abide in God, and God abides in them. (1 JOHN 4:10,16)

At this stage, a reader could well ask what the link is between the idea of love used in connection with God and in peoples' everyday experience. Love between human beings can obviously have a wide range of expressions and meanings. The love a mother has for a child; love and care shown to the sick; love of friends, and sexual or erotic love. What is common to these different expressions of love is the way love brings us out of ourselves and establishes bonds, commitments and fulfilment. The love that we call erotic, flowing from our sexuality, is possibly the most powerful force in life and can either be creative and enhancing or a source of pain and confusion. In a relationship which develops and is personal, erotic love combines with friendship to enable a permanent commitment. What is important to our search to understand mysticism is that the capacity to love among human beings leads to happiness and fulfilment. It ends isolation and is a force towards building community.

The Language of Love

When we examine the writings of mystics, especially in the Christian tradition, it becomes clear that the language of erotic love is an important element in the expression of mystical experience. However, given the fact that Christianity has often seemed to be anti the body and against sexual pleasure this can lead to a sense of paradox.

A way in to resolving the paradox is to go to the Bible, in particular to the Old Testament book the Song of Songs. This book, which is a collection of poems, is in its literal sense a sheer celebration of the passionate love between men and women. The Song of Songs encourages the reader to appreciate the emotional experiences of love. The Song speaks of the joy of physical presence but also it reflects the pain of absence. Another theme is the mutuality of the feelings which draw women and men together. The admiration and yearning of the lovers in these poems is reciprocal and intense. The lovers praise each other's charms and issue passionate invitations to lovemaking. In these invitations, there is no sense of male domination – the woman's voice sounds loud and clear in the poem, ready to initiate as well as to respond to calls to love.

The Song is exuberant in its eroticism. The woman says in her desire for fulfilment in the arms of her lover: 'Let him kiss me with the kisses of his mouth ... We shall praise your love more than wine' (SONG OF SONGS 1:2,4), while the man is clear about his physical intentions, 'May your breasts be the clusters of grapes, your breath sweet scented as apples' (SONG OF SONGS 7:9). The poetry is erotic in its appreciation of sexual love, but there is never a hint of prurience. The poet conveys the feelings linked to love but does not depict clinical acts of lovemaking. The poet is interested in the whole person.

How did this collection of poems, which are sometimes attributed to King Solomon, come be included in the Bible? Well, the rapturous depiction of love between men and women shows that such activity is healthy, natural and good. If a theological warrant is needed to endorse the joy of the poem, then the first chapter of Genesis is the place to look. There in the story of creation we are told creation is 'good ... indeed ... very good'. That goodness includes our sexuality. Genesis also reminds us that the divine image is shown in the complementarity of the male and female. Sexuality is a good gift to be rejoiced in and part of God's design for human life.

> *God created humankind in his image,*
> *in the image of God he created them;*
> *male and female he created them.* (GENESIS 1:27)

While the Song of Songs was intended to celebrate the gift and beauty of sexuality, other meanings were attached to the poem and they will be important in the understanding of mysticism. The Bible, both Old and New Testament, has often used the metaphor of marriage to express the relationship between God and people.

> *As the bridegroom rejoices over the bride,*
> *so shall your God rejoice over you.* (ISAIAH 62:5)

God initiates and maintains a loving relationship with those who accept his invitation. It is in the context of this key metaphor that first Jewish and then Christian teachers began to see the Song of Songs as being capable of expressing the love between God and humankind.

In the Christian tradition, Origen, writing in Alexandria in the second century, saw this love-song as expressing the union of the individual person with Jesus Christ. So the theologian took the poem that celebrates sexuality and gave it a meaning that places love on a different level. But the change of interpretation, or the allegorical meaning, to give it its technical name, leaves the notion of union and intimacy intact. Jesus is now the Lover and the individual Christian is called into an intimacy as intense as a sexual union, but at a level that goes beyond normal categories. But the crux is that such talk of union with the divine is only possible because we know of the reality of the intimacy that comes from our sexuality. If sexuality is perceived as a good gift from God, then it must be seen as crucial in any understanding of God loving us, and vice versa. To deny our sexuality or ignore it is no recipe for closeness to God, and yet much of what passes for Christian morality would take us down that road – that the way to God is to denigrate the body, our feelings and desires.

Origen's writings on the Song of Songs were to have a great influence down the centuries and affected such outstanding figures as Bernard of Clairvaux, Rysbroec (the great Flemish mystic), and Richard Rolle, the English author of *The Cloud of Unknowing*. We know that John of the Cross was drawn to the Song of Songs and it became his favourite Biblical text, so much so that he knew it by heart.

Another word that needs examining in relation to mysticism is 'secret'. In English, secret often means something special or esoteric. Perhaps the meaning that best relates to mysticism is 'a reality that has to be discovered'; it is beyond our normal grasp of things, and yet not irrational or magical. Dionysus, a Syrian theologian from the fifth century, was the first writer to develop this notion. He stressed the secretness or mystery of God. God is light beyond light and this light is usually perceived as darkness. He said this to emphasize his belief that the things of God are beyond the human eye and ear. This echoes the teachings of St Paul and is part of a tradition that asks us to avoid having a set image of God and to be open to the wonderful fullness of God. Rigid images of God can so often be barriers to the reality of God. Sometimes people say they can no longer believe, when in fact what they mean is they have gone beyond seeing God in a particular way.

The mystic is someone who has moved away from images of God to a point when they are open to a loving relation with a God whom they see as personal. The nature of that relationship is intense and beautiful, and often expressed in the language and images of sexual love. The high point of that experience is often described as ecstasy. Ecstasy is a state that occurs when, under the power of love, a person feels that he or she has been raised to a point of union with God. The mystic believes that this is made possible by the action of the divine. It is not a self-induced state, nor does the mystic use any form of drug. It is a state of standing outside oneself to be one with God. St Paul expresses this powerfully when he says, 'I live, now not I, but Christ lives in me' (GALATIANS 2:20).

Ecstasy is also linked to a deep sense of commitment and joy. Again the language of sexual love has to be brought to bear. Once the Beloved (God or Christ) is known then nothing else can satisfy the Lover (the mystic). Everything else in life pales into insignificance. In the gospels, the discovery of God as love is expressed in the parables about treasures and precious pearls. Once the treasure is discovered, nothing else matters, the only way forward is to sell everything and gain the treasure, the pearl beyond price. John of the Cross uses the words *nada* (nothing) and *toda* (all) in this context. For John even though his life was full of many and varied activities all of these were *nada* before the utter loveliness and wonder of the deep loving experiences of God that came into his life. God became all (*toda*) for John.

John believed, as all mystics do, that God gave him the gift of loving knowledge. He trusted, he believed that all this is possible. In the Christian tradition, this is what is called faith. It is, at heart, a sense of loving trust in God, in God's promise and what God can do in our humanity. However, while faith in God might not be easily acceptable today faith, trust among human beings is crucial to life. We trust people in so many ways, from our parents to our lovers, or to those who do practical things on our behalf. We have faith in the train driver, or the engineer who designed the bridge we are driving over.

It is commonplace to claim that we live in an era almost devoid of faith, but is that really the case? In the past, the social and cultural climate was favourable to belief in God. There was a community of values between art, science and religion. Dante, Shakespeare, Newton and Beethoven believed in values over and above their work. Today it would seem that nothing can be certain and that all values are relative. However, is that the full picture or is there a liberal establishment saying one thing while there are still many people who would be willing to risk believing? Perhaps it would be more realistic to say that right across society there are still many who believe in God and many more who would like to be helped to come to a sense of a personal God. Is the mystic someone who could speak lovingly to modern men and women, speaking of experiences that could resonate in their feelings, in their imaginations?

John the Poet

John of the Cross can certainly address our imagination because he expressed his deep religious experiences in poetry. He found a poetic voice which sang beautifully of his intimate experiences.

John had shown a great love for poems, songs and music when he worked in the hospital at Medina. He had a gift of easing the pain of patients by singing songs which he had composed. This gift seemed to go underground when he studied theology but was given a new lease of life by Teresa of Avila, who wanted him to break out of his seriousness. Teresa herself was no mean poet and she often challenged John to cap some poem she had written.

However, it was his experience of imprisonment at Toledo in 1577–8 that gave rise to his great poetic outpouring. The intensity of his suffering and his simultaneous awareness of God's love and goodness gave birth to an amazing lyric voice in John.

John's love of poetry had its roots in the popular songs he heard as a boy in Medina. Medina was famous for its market and the crowds were entertained by singers with their repertoire of love-songs. John also had a chance to study literature, first of all at the Jesuit College and then during the noviciate. He would have read the great Latin poets, such as Horace and Ovid, and also the poems of a contemporary Spanish poet, Garcilaso de la Vega. Garcilaso was a young man about the Spanish Court who cut rather an heroic figure. He died young, but his poems were full of invention and innovation. John was obviously impressed with his work, especially the sensitive way he wrote of nature. John loved nature and felt a kinship with Garcilaso's imaginative approach.

John's poetic output is not huge. In fact the totality of his works comes to about 40 pages in *The Collected Works*. His poetry dates from 1578, with 'The Spiritual Canticle' being among the earliest of his works, and with 'The Living Flame of Love', written in 1585, rounding off his poetic output.

Rather than talking about and around John's poetry it would be better to let John speak for himself. For this purpose, the poem 'The Dark Night' would be a good choice. The text and translation comes from *The Collected Works of St John of the Cross*, edited and translated by Kieran Kavanaugh and Otilio Rodriguez.

NOCHE OSCURA
Canciones de el alma que se goza de haber llegado al alto esta-
do de la perfección, que es la unión con Dios, por el camino de
la negación espiritual.

I
En una noche oscura,
con ansias, en amores inflamada,
¡oh dichosa ventura!
salí sin ser notada
estando ya mi casa sosegada.

II
A oscuras y segura,
por la secreta escala disfrazada,
¡oh dichosa ventura!
a oscuras y en celada,
estando ya mi casa sosegada.

III
En la noche dichosa,
en secreto, que nadie me veía,
ni yo miraba cosa,
sin otra luz y guía
sino la que en el corazón ardía.

IV
Aquésta me guiaba
más cierto que la luz del mediodía,
adónde me esperaba
quien yo bien me sabía,
en parte donde nadie parecía.

V
¡Oh noche que guiaste!
¡Oh noche amable más que el alborada!
¡Oh noche que juntaste
Amado con amada,
amada en el Amado transformada!

VI
En mi pecho florido,
que entero para él solo se guardaba,
allí quedó dormido,
y yo le regalaba,
y el ventalle de cedros aire daba.

VII
El aire de la almena,
cuando yo sus cabellos esparcía,
con su mano serena
en mi cuello hería
y todos mis sentidos suspendía.

VIII
Quedéme y olvidéme,
el rostro recliné sobre el Amado,
cesó todo y dejéme,
dejando me cuidado
entre las azucenas olvidado.

THE DARK NIGHT
Songs of the soul that rejoices in having reached the high
state of perfection, which is union with God, by the path of
spiritual negation.

I
One dark night,
fired with love's urgent longings
– ah, the sheer grace! –
I went out unseen,
my house being now all stilled.

II
In darkness, and secure,
by the secret ladder, disguised,
– ah, the sheer grace! –
in darkness and concealment,
my house being now all stilled.

III

On that glad night
in secret, for no one saw me,
nor did I look at anything
with no other light or guide
than the one that burned in my heart.

IV

This guided me
more surely than the light of noon
to where he was awaiting me
– him I knew so well –
there in a place where no one appeared.

V

O guiding night!
O night more lovely than the dawn!
O night that has united
the Lover with his beloved,
transforming the beloved in her Lover.

VI

Upon my flowering breast,
which I kept wholly for him alone,
there he lay sleeping,
and I caressing him
there in a breeze from the fanning cedars.

VII

When the breeze blew from the turret,
as I parted his hair,
it wounded my neck
with its gentle hand,
suspending all my senses.

VIII
I abandoned and forgot myself,
laying my face on my Beloved;
all things ceased; I went out from myself,
leaving my cares
forgotten among the lilies.

John wrote this poem in the months after his escape from Toledo. It is rich in symbolism and, while a translation can never capture the power of the original poem, there is more than enough to enjoy. The poem uses the symbol of night in a way that draws out a sense of mystery. The night recalls the darkness of John's prison cell and the times of darkness when he must have been torn by a range of conflicting emotions. Was he in prison because he was at fault? Why had his own turned against him? But night is also a time of mystery when deep feelings can well up, a time to begin a journey.

In fact, the opening stanza, which rejoices in the freedom of the Lover to leave the house, echoes the Song of Songs:

Upon my bed at night
I sought him whom my soul loves;
I sought him, but found him not ...
'I will rise now and go about the city ...
I will seek him whom my soul loves.' (SONG OF SONGS 3:1–2)

Because the Lover feels so passionately, the night is no longer a threat – the rapturous love inside her soul is like a light. The light in her heart is a better guide than a full moon. The burning love is not only a light but it seems like a guiding, homing beacon as she finds her Beloved. In stanza V, John introduces a new symbolic element as the poem sings of the night in language that echoes the great Easter hymn of light, the *Exsultet*. Stanza V begins:

O guiding night!
O night more lovely than the dawn!

while the *Exsultet* proclaims:

Of this night scripture says:
The night will be as clear as day:
it will become my light, my joy.

In stanza VI of 'The Dark Night', the Beloved rests and sleeps on the Lover's breast because the purification has been so complete that it has become the most fitting place for union and in that closeness the wound of union takes place. The union is beyond anything the senses can begin to describe or comprehend. The union is also expressed as a wound, as the immensity of love is painful to the human spirit as the finite is overwhelmed by the infinite. So it feels a pain at being unable to take in such love in its entirety. This is a state which Teresa of Avila also experiences and describes in her writings.

So the Lover, who stands for you and I as we journey to God, has found perfect union with God. The final stanza takes us to fulfilment and hints at the joy of heaven, the beatific vision. This state of union where only God matters is the mystic state, and John maintains that human beings can experience such closeness to God in this life. The poem, as it moves from the house to finding the Beloved, expresses a journey that is a wonderful risk. Perhaps John is trying to tell us that because we perceive the image of God in our humanity, then if we trust enough in who we are we can be passionately close to God. This sense of trust is implied in the closing lines:

I went out from myself,
leaving my cares
forgotten among the lilies.

These lines link the poem by allusion to the Sermon on the Mount, where Christ uses the beauty of the lilies of the field to emphasise God's care for us and our need to trust in that care:

'Consider the lilies of the field, how they grow; they neither toil nor spin, yet I tell you, even Solomon in all his glory was not clothed like one of these.' (MATTHEW 6:28–29)

The technique behind 'The Dark Night' warrants examination and provides insights into the way John crafted his experiences. John once told a friend that when he tried to compose poetry, 'Sometimes God gave me words and sometimes I looked for them myself.' Obviously, a good working knowledge of Spanish is needed to appreciate the details of John's art, but with the help of translation the essence of the poems can still be touched.

What is obvious is the simplicity of the language. Adjectives are few, but the nouns and verbs carefully chosen – all have force. The word 'night' appears and reappears, growing richer and richer in meaning. It begins as the night that enables the Lover to start on the quest; gradually, by the third stanza, it is linked to joy, and by the fifth stanza it has become the means for the lovers' union. In the same stanza, there's the marvellous way the union is described – at once economical and also allowing the force of the words to underline the marvel.

Amado con amada,	*The Lover with his beloved,*
amada en el Amado transformada!	*transforming the beloved in her Lover.*

The reader just has to say the Spanish aloud to get the feeling of the union taking place, the very sound conveys a sense of amazing communion of ecstatic love.

Other Poems

One of the poems which John brought out of prison was a song of rejoicing in knowing God through faith. 'For I know well the spring that flows and runs, although it is night.' For John, this is an eternal spring with an unknown origin, full of beauty and abundance. On an obvious level, the fountain is the source of hope that kept John going while he was in prison. It could also be the river Tagus that ran close by, becoming a memory of freedom and life for someone cooped up in the savage Castilian climate. Fountains, of course, bring pastoral memories, places where lovers meet, and such images from romantic poetry would have echoed in John's mind. However, as a Carmelite, John would have remembered a classic text that was part of his formation, *The Institutions of the First Monks*. The author, the Catalan Philip Ribot, writes of Carmelite origins and envisages the life of the hermits on Carmel. The early Carmelites living on Mount Carmel lived by the fount of the prophet Elijah. Elijah was the one who drank from the abundance of the torrent Kerith in time of drought. Drinking from the torrent in this text is a metaphor for intimate union with God. It is a description of mystical experience, one which Carmelites down the ages were told could be part of their life, their prayer.

Besides all this – and part of the richness of John's work in allowing his memory to be quarried for his poems – are the allusions to the Scriptures. John evokes rather than quotes, and allows his various allusions to grow like a tapestry. Again, all of this was a creative process taking place in confinement, with memory as the sole source. The living and ever more powerful source of water echoes the visions of the prophet Ezekiel, but more than anything, the reader is aware of imagery inspired by the gospel according to John. The living waters and the living bread speak of baptism and eucharist, and the texture of the poem is at times dominated by Joannine themes. 'This eternal fountain is concealed from sight within this living bread to give us life' (CF. JOHN 4:7–15 AND 6:41–51).

Another prison poem is a ballad based on Psalm 137, 'By The Rivers of Babylon'. The prison in Toledo has become John's Babylon, his place of exile, and yet he lives in hope and trust. While he is in this harsh place he undergoes an amazing purification, as if by fire. Love strikes, and in the process of wounding him John finds that love is actually taking his heart over:

There love wounded me
and took away my heart.

This paradox is carried to a further stage:

I died within myself for you,
and for you I revived.

Here, John is echoing St Paul's teaching that those who come to know Christ want to die to anything that could separate them from God's love, and only want the new life that is Christ. John wants to risk everything to gain the great treasure – God. As he composes this poem in prison, John is realizing how radical the process of reaching real freedom is – the freedom to be really open to God.

'The Spiritual Canticle'

The great poem of his imprisonment in Toledo is 'The Spiritual Canticle'. The first 31 stanzas were written in prison and the last eight were added between 1579 and 1584. The 'Canticle' expresses the deep mystical experience that came out of John's time in prison. The expression of what, on one level, could be beyond words comes from John's memories, his subconscious and his deep knowledge of Scripture. An insight into the poem's composition from the twentieth century could help us understand the creative process behind this and other of John's prison poems. The various Beirut hostages, victims of the Lebanese conflict, kept themselves sane by reciting poems they remembered from child-hood or told themselves stories from whatever source their memories provided.

John gives this poem the subtitle: 'Songs between the soul and the Bridegroom'. The soul, the Bride, is called the Lover who searches for the Beloved who is Christ. The first two stanzas set the scene and also show the influences behind the poem.

I

BRIDE   *Where have you hidden,*
Beloved, and left me moaning?
You fled like the stag
after wounding me;
I went out calling you, but you were gone.

II

Shepherds, you who go
up through the sheepfolds to the hill,
if by chance you see
him I love most,
tell him I am sick, I suffer, and I die.

The obvious influence is the Song of Songs, but what matters is the way John uses and transforms his material. The opening stanza reflects the conflict going on inside John in prison. He loves God and yet feels deserted. He has loved God as fiercely as any human lover and yet feels lost, alone. The wound is the wound of love and also a sense of loss. Who knows that during his imprisonment John did not go through a time of darkness and shock? Why was he misunderstood? At such times, fear, and perhaps even doubt about his relationship with God, pressed in on him. These two stanzas can operate on various levels of interpretation, but they are in one sense a great cry of pain from John, feeling abandoned and confused in his prison cell.

However, if the poem is John's reworking of the Song of Songs as an ecstatic poem, helping us to have images of the mystical, then the cry is the expression of the deepest desire for God. In this context, the wounding is not some pain inflicted by God but the sensation a human being has when exposed to fullness of God. Wounding is, for John, the sensation of ecstatic prayer, as it was for St Teresa. There is a famous statue by Bernini (1598–1680) that represents St Teresa of Avila in ecstasy, where Teresa is seen with arms outstretched while an angel pierces her heart with a spear.

The setting for the lovers' search is pastoral with shepherds and beautiful rolling countryside. The Lover is distraught and over-whelmed by the beauty and power of the Beloved, so much so that it seems that she can no longer survive. She cries:

Reveal your presence,
and may the vision of your beauty be my death

Then the beautiful stanza:

O spring like crystal!
If only, on your silvered-over faces,
you would suddenly form
the eyes I have desired,
that I bear sketched deep within my heart.

The Beloved appears, and the sense of union begins to emerge, with image after image impacting to create the joy of union with God. The Beloved is everything marvellous in nature and the Lover, having drunk of the wine, feels freedom. The Beloved giving his heart makes the Lover his bride and the soul is now totally given to the Beloved.

For now I practise love and love alone

The Lover knows that the Beloved is enthralled with her because even the hairs on the nape of her neck seem fascinating. This whimsical and yet deeply erotic image points up just how much God is involved with us. The next image shows how God's gazing on us changes us because we become imprinted with the grace and loveliness of the Divine. One of the most memorable images of the sheer delight and play that exist in a deep relationship between God and the one loved is in the following stanza.

Catch us the foxes,
for our vineyard is now in flower,
while we fashion a cone of roses
intricate as the pine's
and let no one appear on the hill.

Then the Bride enters into the long-desired and pleasant garden, lying at ease resting in the Beloved's gentle arms.

Fulfilment, rest, joy and peace. The apple tree is now a place of healing, in contrast to the tree in Eden. The garden image is both pastoral and biblical, but also a special one for John. Carmel means 'the Garden of the Lord', a space for God, and John's work in the Reform was to create true Carmels, true Gardens of the Lord. During his years of founding communities, one of his joys was to design and create gardens, places where friars and nuns could have space to enjoy the beauty of nature and find God. So it is no accident that the joy of union is found in the garden.

'The Living Flame of Love'

The last of the poems to be considered is 'The Living Flame of Love'. This was composed in Granada between 1582 and 1584. The poem and the subsequent commentary were written for Doña Ana y Peñalosa, a devout laywoman that John directed. The poem and the commentary speak of the summit of mystical experience.

The poem is in a different form, having six rather than five lines per stanza, and it has a sense of ascending movement, like a dance. It is full of cries:

Oh llama de amor viva ...	*O living flame of love ...*
Oh cauterio suave	*O Sweet cautery,*
Oh regalada llaga ...	*O delightful wound! ...*
Oh mano blanda	*O gentle hand!*
Oh toque delicado ...	*O delicate touch ...*
Oh lamparas de fuego ...	*O lamps of fire! ...*

The ecstasy is both painful and yet delightful. The wound, the burn hurts yet it is sweet and delicate, the hand is soft. The poem shows the paradox of comfort coming with pain and the sense of healing as the one searching for God goes beyond a certain stage.

The phrase 'lamps of fire' is also evocative of the Spirit coming down as tongues of fire (CF. ACTS 2:1-4). For John, in this poem, the one who is in union with the Beloved is also united with the Spirit, the bond of love between Christ and the Father. The Spirit is a living flame, but is also love and a comforter. It is because John, in expressing his sense of deepest union with God, takes us into the life of the Christian God who is one and yet three, that he begins to find communication difficult. He is looking into mystery which for him is reality and yet at the same time, beyond the grasp of reason and intelligence. Language reaches breaking point, and so the language of the poem, with its cries and a seeming absence of verbs, proclaims that a boundary has been reached. Perhaps this is why John changes from five to six lines per stanza, to hint at the abundance of the Spirit. John now realizes that his union with the Beloved, with Christ, is possible because the love of God is at work in him, effecting a painful and yet loving transformation.

Transformed, John is able to rest with the Beloved and experience what St Augustine hoped for in his famous saying, 'my heart shall be restless till it rests in thee'. In this poem, John shows us that under the influence of the Spirit, the event the great Augustine thought impossible can happen even in this life. Our humanity, because of its origins in God, is apt for union with God when we open ourselves in trust to our creator.

Reading John's poems, with their powerful descriptions of the mystic state, the union of a human being with God, the question that confronts us is: Where does all this fit in with contemporary experience? The twentieth century is a century that has witnessed sexual revolution, bringing with it a new freedom in talking about and expressing human sexuality. In that context, John's poems have something to say about the value and power of erotic interpersonal love. If the reality of erotic love gives the mystic images and a language to express the relation between the divine and human, then conversely the mystic wants to tell modern men and women to look again at their sexuality and their sexual relations. The mystic would want people today to place a high value on sexual intimacy and to value it as the highest possible form of communication, in which the whole person should be affirmed and enhanced. In the spirit of the Book of Genesis, John's poetry speaks to us today of the goodness of creation, the goodness of sexuality.

3

The Prose Works

John of the Cross wrote four great prose works which began as commentaries on his poems but in reality they provide his vision of how we achieve union with God. The four works are *The Ascent of Mount Carmel*, *The Dark Night*, *The Spiritual Canticle* and *The Living Flame of Love*. They were written between 1579 and 1586 and were meant to help friars and nuns of the Discalced Reform in their relationship to God. John, therefore, was writing for people who were committed to an ever closer union with God and were ready to be challenged by what he had to say. He usually knew the people he was writing for and felt free to be himself in what he said. Again, we must remember that the temperament of sixteenth-century Spaniards was vigorous – willing to be stretched and not satisfied with compromise. It is a whole mental universe away from the modern world, with its uncertainties and the need for most of life to be on the level of instant gratification. It was a world of faith, and for these nuns and friars, their Carmelite Rule presented the following of Christ as a core value.

John wrote in a plain, direct way. He did not indulge in flowery, rhetorical writing. There are frequent quotations from the Bible and, of course, there is the influence of scholastic theology and philosophy. Aquinas and Augustine are the theologians who formed his world view. However, what does make his prose works difficult are his long parentheses. He can be very wordy at times, wandering off his subject and leaving the reader quite bewildered. A sentence can end up being a paragraph long, and John was well aware of this tendency. Another problem was the fact that he often broke off from writing because of the various responsibilities he had in the Reform. When he came back to the text he would often retrace his steps, treating the same material twice over in slightly differing ways.

At this stage it would be helpful to have an overview of the prose works and then look at the key concepts in greater detail.

The Ascent of Mount Carmel is closely linked to *The Dark Night*. John wrote these treatises between 1579 and 1584 and their focus is his poem, 'The Dark Night'.

The text of *The Ascent of Mount Carmel* is prefaced by a sketch of Mount Carmel or the Mount of Perfection. It was originally drawn for the nuns at Beas, but copies were made for the friars in Baeza and Granada. It is meant to be a summary of the book and the verses that accompany it express the antithesis between *todo* (all) and *nada* (nothing) which is at the core of his thinking. This antithesis can seem off-putting, but in fact *nada*, or nothing, is part of a process that achieves deep personal freedom – the off-loading of baggage that prevents personal growth. The way of *nada* is part of the journey called the dark night.

Nada is not meant to imply anything life denying nor does it mean putting the created into second place. It is meant to be positive, it is about genuine growth. However, this journey is something John will explain in detail. At this stage, it is useful to compare the journey with gospel images. The way to God is by the narrow path or the narrow gateway, the broad highway is not the way to go (CF. MATTHEW 7:13-14).

John refers to four different 'nights', which are all phases of the dark night of faith by which the soul journeys to union with God. John's analysis is built on two pairs of terms: **sense** and **spirit**; **active** and **passive**.

The active night of the sense can be initiated by anyone who wants to be closer to God. This night consists essentially in correcting obviously sinful behaviour and self-centred gratification.

The movement from **the active night of the spirit** to **the passive night of the sense** is a movement from meditation to contemplative prayer. It is also a time when obvious consolations associated with prayer fade away and the individual is challenged to live by faith and to let God take control.

The passive night of the spirit is a final purification which leads to deep mystical experience. It demands patience and is a slow process. The individual can feel powerless, crushed; everything seems dark. It is as if God has abandoned the individual concerned. The other side of this night is mystical union.

John's ordered treatment of the 'nights' does not mean that everyone has to come to union with God in this precise way. It is important to remember that this scheme is not an absolute. It is something that takes place inside someone open to God. Therefore the teaching on the night only makes sense when we respect the uniqueness of the person and remember that God's action in our lives has a freedom and gratuitous quality that can never be analysed or predicted.

The Ascent was written after John had experienced such close union with God, first of all in prison, and then in the time that followed that harrowing period. He had journeyed and now, on the summit, he could see the best way to travel and wanted to share the joy he had found. He was also aware that there were many people who desired closeness with God but had no guides. He wanted, therefore, to give people solid, substantial doctrine to help them.

John introduces the concept of the dark night immediately as the way a person grows closer to God. He points out that what he has to say will not be easy and apologizes for his 'awkward style'. He stresses he is writing for people who are already taking all this very seriously – the friars and nuns of the Reform.

It needs to be made quite clear that John saw the dark night as being initiated by God, but that does not mean that the individual concerned is totally passive in the process. Another aspect of the dark night is the way a person so affected has the feeling that God seems to be absent, it is important to recognize that this is a seeming absence of God. It is not as if God has withdrawn from a person's life. Again it needs to be noted that not everyone in their journey to God passes through the 'dark night'. In an attempt to understand what John means by the 'dark night', the reader must always remember that the person who has entered this process has to play his or her part. John would not want to deny our basic freedom or our use of reason.

The 'dark night' is, then, a freeing of desires so that the individual is not caught up with lesser gods; this in a way is a joy and a gift from God. John is anxious that his reader's way of living is not habitually fixed on realities that would eclipse God. Creation is good, but it is the way we use it that matters and it is important to live under the rule of Christ's love to give life its proper focus. John then shows in Book I, Chapter XIII, that following Christ must be everything if the necessary purification is to be achieved. Echoing the Carmelite Rule, he stresses the need to reflect on Christ's life as found in the Scriptures. It is in that love for Christ, who is at the centre of our lives, that we gain the motivation to rid ourselves of desires and ways of living that are not open to God.

Books II and III are dominated by John's reflections on faith. For John, faith or the life of faith is a 'dark night'. Dark because it is beyond intelligence and the intellect is not equipped to cope with its light. It is like a night animal whose eyes are attuned to the dark but then cannot cope with the brightness of daylight. Faith is directed to Christ, who is light – this sense of Christ as light is a powerful image in the gospel of John. It is in this context then that union with God can happen, because a person becomes open to the possibility of loving knowledge – wisdom being communicated to the core of one's being.

John also makes the point that while union with Christ is the goal of this active purification, we all reach it in an individual manner, a way special to each one of us. An interesting aspect of

John's teaching is the way he wants to ground this faith journey in the life of the Church and how much he values the role of reason, not wanting people to go running off looking for apparitions and miraculous statues. He sees the restlessness implied in such activity as running counter to what matters, which is putting all one's energy into the union with Christ. John was conscious that in a society that was by and large illiterate, there was a danger that people could bestow magical properties on statues or paintings. For John, the Church in its teaching role had to call for objectivity in these matters. The phenomenon of weeping or miraculous statues is still common today, and bishops often become unpopular when they caution people against credulity.

The theological virtues – faith, hope and charity – are seen as crucial by John in the work of purification.

The intellect must be perfected in the darkness of faith, the memory in the emptiness of hope and the will in the nakedness and absence of every affection.

For John, these virtues empty the person of all that is not God and help prayer life to grow simple, moving from words and concepts to a sense of intimate friendship. *The Ascent* finishes abruptly since, for myriad reasons, John found he could not move onto the next area of teaching which concerned him – the passive purification. John saw the passive purification as the special way God acted on the human person so that radical growth could take place in the core of that person. In terms of commenting on the poem *The Ascent* only touches on two stanzas!

The Passive Night

The Dark Night covers material that John had wanted to deal with in *The Ascent* but never managed to achieve, namely the passive purification. It looks at God's action on the human person. John claims that in this commentary he will be more faithful to the poem itself. He is, to a great degree, but ends the work with a comment on the first line of only the third stanza. John is most interested in sharing the experience expressed in the first two stanzas of the poem. He wants to tell his readers of the joy of union with God and how he has escaped from all the negative aspects of his personality to reach that stage.

The commentary combines personal experience along with theological reflection. Book I looks at the passive night of the senses while Book II examines the passive night of the spirit. John makes it clear that while much of the journeying to full union with God is the result of divine action, this does not mean that the individual has nothing to contribute. It is a principle of Catholic theology that all the work of people being saved, achieving union with God involves human co-operation. While it is true that human nature is finite or limited, that does not mean it cannot be open to God, to the divine working on the human. What human beings have to do is to be willing to be open to God, and then God will achieve wonderful things in the individual. St Paul expresses the action of God on humanity in the letter to the Ephesians: 'Glory be to him whose power, working in us, can do infinitely more than we can ask or imagine' (EPHESIANS 3:20).

The signs of the passive night of the senses are:

1 There is no sense of consolation present in any aspect of life, definitely no consolation from prayer.
2 Trying to serve God but getting nowhere and feeling that they are far from God. The reason for this is that God is trying to move us from feeling good about God to a deeper awareness.

3 A movement from meditation to contemplative prayer. In other
   words the agenda for prayer comes from God, not methods and
   modes of our choosing.

The passive night of the spirit is described in Chapter IV of the
Book II. Here, a new way of loving and understanding is achieved.
The intellect, purified by God, no longer operates under its own
vigour but by means of divine wisdom. The act of loving, which,
for John, is rooted in the will, now comes from the action of the
Holy Spirit. John sees this as the loving wisdom of God which
purges and illumines a human being and prepares us for union
with God. All of this is painful because it goes beyond our normal
way of thinking and of being in control. The letting go, allowing
God to have the initiative, brings a new freedom and a new sense
of the presence of God through faith and love.

Again, John finished the commentary when he felt he had
done all he could to help his readers. The rest is for us to apply to
our personal situations. Let John speak as the commentary con-
cludes:

*Love alone, which at this period burns by soliciting the heart for the
Beloved, is what guides and moves her, and makes her soar to God in
an unknown way along the road of solitude.*

Mystical Understanding

The commentary on *The Spiritual Canticle* was written at the re-
quest of Mother Ana de Jesus, Prioress of the Discalced Carmelite
nuns at St Joseph's in Granada, in 1584. Ana de Jesús was one of
the great figures of the Carmelite Reform and a person of deep
faith and commitment. She was a close friend of John of the
Cross, having known him since 1575. In the latter part of her life
she went on to France and Belgium where she founded a number
of convents.

The fact that the commentary was written for the nuns at Granada indicates a high level of interest and understanding. The community under their idealistic superior would have been eager for help in their own lives. John often came to give talks to the community, finding them willing listeners, and it is out of this context that the commentary was born.

Contemporary sources show the nuns found the poem dazzling in its imagery and beauty. They would have recognized the links with the Song of Songs and known that the poem was an expression in lyric form of John's profound experience.

John states his intentions quite openly, almost naïvely, in writing in the prologue to the commentary.

> *These stanzas Reverend Mother were obviously composed with a certain burning love of God. The wisdom and charity of God is so vast, as the Book of Wisdom states, that it reaches from end to end [WISDOM 8:1] and the soul informed and moved by it bears in some way this very abundance and impulsiveness in her words ... It would be foolish to think that expressions of love arising from mystical understanding, like these stanzas, are fully explainable. The Spirit of the Lord, who abides in us and aids our weakness, as St Paul says [ROMANS 8:26] pleads for us with unspeakable groanings in order to manifest what we can neither fully understand nor comprehend.*

John goes on to say that detailed explanations are not possible as 'the abundant meanings of the Holy Spirit cannot be caught in words'. Again, John makes the point that the commentary aims to shed some light on the poem as he is conscious that the 'stanzas were composed in a love flowing from abundant mystical understanding'. Finally, John apologizes for using scholastic theology as a means of expression, even though he knows it could well be off-putting. John would have been aware that by using too much technical language he would have lost half of his readers. The Carmelite Friars who studied academic theology would have been conversant with such language, but the nuns would not have had access to university faculties. John would be delighted to see in the twentieth century that men and women had equal opportunities in these areas.

There is one problematic factor with John's commentary. Two editions of the commentary are extant. The first or A text is favoured by Fr Lucien, a French Carmelite who writes on John in *La Dictionnaire de Spiritualité*, and by many other experts, including Gerald Brenan in his perceptive work, *St John of the Cross: his life and poetry*. However, Kieran Kavanaugh of the American Carmelite school favours the B text, in the edition of John of the Cross's works published in 1991 by the Institute of Carmelite Studies, Washington. There is an important difference between the two editions. The A text follows the original shape of the poem, where the intimate union with the Lover and the Beloved takes place in this life. The B text alters the order of the stanzas, suggesting the fullness of union between the Lover and Beloved as being a reality that occurs in the Beatific Vision, in other words in the next life.

Why did the changes take place and what importance can be read into the new edition? Perhaps John made the changes as a result of conversations with the nuns, or perhaps he was anxious that his ideas, once they were in the public forum, could be criticized by the Inquisition. Whatever the reason, many experts would favour the A text because it allows for a greater optimism about the possibility of an intimacy with God in this life. It would indicate a sense that our human nature working with God can achieve the sublime here and now.

In some ways, the commentary on the 'Canticle' is disappointing. John admits in the prologue that his poem comes from love and mystical experience. Once he starts to explain this and that aspect of the work, there is a feeling that the poem is being dragged down. There is a whole world of difference between inspiration and interpretation. Another problem arises out of John's need to see or explain everything as allegorical so that mountains for instance stand for virtues. The poem is beyond allegory, it is stating a deeply personal experience. It is about love at its most sublime.

The 'Canticle', if it can be explained, must be seen in the light of its relationship to the Song of Songs, but even then there are complexities. John had so made the biblical text part of his life that the Song of Songs was part of his mind's eye and would have influenced his poetry and been quarried at a subliminal level. It was like the air he breathed.

The commentary, then, needs to be seen in its context – a guidebook to help the nuns he loved so much both achieve the joy of union with God and avoid pitfalls along the way. His friend St Teresa would in these circumstances have written a treatise. John prefers a commentary on his poem, but in the end the poem rather than the commentary is the best guide.

Spiritual Marriage

Both the poem 'The Living Flame of Love' and the prose commentary were written for Doña Ana y Peñalosa. Doña Ana, a widow, lived in Granada, and when the first Carmelite nuns came to Granada, Doña Ana allowed them to use her house until their convent was ready. Doña Ana became a close friend of Ana de Jesús, the Prioress, and subsequently got to know John of the Cross. John of the Cross was to become the guide of this generous woman who wanted help in her prayer life. It was quite unusual for a laywoman to be helped in this way, but it was a case of two generous people meeting. At the time, the whole question of meditation and contemplative prayer was under scrutiny by the Spanish Inquisition. This body, anxious to preserve both Church and national unity, was always suspicious of anything that was not initiated by the institutional Church. Gifted people like John could and did come under investigation as there were always people who could be jealous. It is interesting to note that when John does go public in his commentaries he is very careful to show modesty and deference to the Church's authority:

> *Only the faults and mistakes of this commentary will be mine. Submitting it to the judgement and better opinion of our Holy Mother the Roman Catholic Church, by whose rule no one errs, finding my support in Sacred Scripture.*

John was not a person who sought any conflict with the Church authorities. However, misunderstanding often arises when people bent on bureaucratic action examine the work of someone gifted. The functionary can be well-versed in law but perhaps fails to recognize the depth and beauty of the visionary. In our present era, great Christian thinkers like Yves Conger and Teilhard de Chardin have been misunderstood. John had to cope with people who were on the defensive, suspicious of anything that was out of the ordinary.

In the commentary on 'The Living Flame of Love', John treats each stanza of the poem in detail. In many ways what he writes is a continuation of his teaching about the possibility of perfect union with God, or Spiritual Marriage. In *The Spiritual Canticle*, John describes Spiritual Marriage as:

> *a total transformation in the Beloved in which each surrenders the entire possession of self to the other ... The soul becomes divine, becomes God through participation in so far as it is possible in this life.*

St Paul expressed the intimacy of this union when he says: 'I live, now not I, but Christ lives in me' (GALATIANS 2:20). At the core of *The Living Flame* is the activity of the Holy Spirit, the flame. For John, people purified by the flame live even now on the threshold of eternal life. The action of the Spirit seems to be ready to take us out of this life.

With ardent desire the soul tells the flame the Holy Spirit to tear the veil of mortal life now by that sweet encounter in which he truly communicates entirely what he is ... That is complete and perfect glory.

John stresses in this work the glory that the human person can encounter, and the beauty of the relationship that is possible with the triune God, Father, Son and Spirit. Faith is no longer dark, the veil is almost transparent and light floods in. In short, a state of perfect love has been achieved.

John wrote this commentary over quite a short period, in between carrying out his varied tasks as a superior in the Reform. In the last months of his life he revised the texts influenced by his prayer life, eager to tell people that God has amazing gifts for those who turn to him with all their being.

Letters

No account of John's prose works would be complete without reference to his letters. We have only 33 of his letters. The reason there are so few is that a campaign of vilification was mounted against John in the last years of his life. The climate of fear that was generated and the ever present reality of the Inquisition caused friends and disciples to destroy his letters. We know that, but for a change of climate in the Reform following John's death, it was possible that all of his works could have been lost. As it was, his works were viewed with suspicion until Clement X declared him blessed in 1675 and Benedict XIII canonized him in 1726.

The letters that remain, and sadly there is no correspondence with his mother and brother, show John as a loving, tender person. Some commentators have seen John as austere and negative, yet nothing could be further from the truth. Many of his letters are meant to help nuns and friars as they journeyed to God, but the tone is warm, immediate – as if he were there in the room talking. At times he shows how much he misses people when he has to

move to different tasks in different parts of Spain. He also gives
advice on business, especially when he sees the nuns being treated
unfairly. He is not beyond telling them to give businessmen a dose
of their own medicine! He also warns the Prioress of Cordoba
against having strict observance for its own sake.

Two letters survive written to Doña Ana y Peñalosa in August
and September 1591, shortly before his death. John is living in the
remote Priory of Peñuela and describes something of his life and
feelings.

*This morning we have already returned from gathering our chickpeas
and so the mornings go by. On another day we shall thresh them. It
is nice to handle these mute creatures, better than being badly han-
dled by living ones. God grant that I may stay here. Pray for this, my
daughter. But even though I am so happy here, I would not fail to
come should you desire.*

These comments are an amazing insight into the feelings of a
loving man, free to express his emotions and obviously valuing his
friendship with Doña Ana. John particularly valued friendship
more and more as he grew older. Why? Because as he experienced
closeness to God he became more fully aware of his own worth
and the worth of others. He was, in the language of his poetry, free
to leave the house and to go out finding love from God and his
contemporaries.

In September he received a packet of letters from Doña Ana.
Already his last illness is overtaking him. He has a slight bout of
fever that means he has to visit Ubeda for medicine. He ends the
letter: 'I am closing on account of the fever, for I would like to write
at greater length'.

The last letter we have of John's is a fragment from a letter
written to a nun in Segovia whose identity is unknown. John was
writing only days before his death and these words say so much
about the man and his message.

Have a great love for those who contradict and fail to love you, for in this way love is begotten in a heart that has no love. God so acts with us, for he loves us that we might love by means of the very love he bears towards us.

4

Nada, the Night and
the Twentieth Century

John of the Cross was shaped by his experience of being a Spaniard living at a time of change. Spain in the sixteenth century was a great power, but it was also a country of extremes and a definite fierceness. However, John was moulded by elements that transcend time and place: his Christian faith and the Carmelite tradition. What then does John have to say today to twentieth-century people, be they friars, nuns, or anyone seeking meaning in life?

To understand John of the Cross, we have to see him to some degree in the context of his time and we also have to acknowledge the influence of his scholastic formation. However, while John's intellectual framework may have been superseded, his writings do relate to the perennial in human nature. What is basic in John is basic to Christianity. John wants each person to allow God to be God for them, a God of love, of freedom, one who is turned towards the human race and asks that people relate to him and each other. It is in the context of this love of God that all of John's teaching about *nada,* the night and purification has its foundation. John proclaims the personal God of the Bible, the God of Abraham, Isaac and Joseph, the God revealed in Jesus Christ.

John of the Cross is like the prophets of the Old Testament in so far as he was impelled to proclaim the living God, and to show that there is no other God and the only way is God's way. Anything else or any other way for John is idolatry. In this he is like Elijah of old, who destroyed Jezebel's idols and journeyed to Mount Horeb where he encountered the living God (CF. 1 KINGS 18,19).

However, in the twentieth century, the denial of God is more common than his proclamation. Alongside this we find men and women filled or rather overwhelmed by uncertainty. The problem of the modern world is that nothing seems certain and, as a result, the transcendent is unthinkable. The rejection of God seems to go hand in hand with the rejection of our fellow human beings. The only relationship that seems consistent is my fascination with my computer and the hope that the next package will give me a window on reality I have never known before. But the computer is only an extension of myself and if anything it absorbs me to such a degree that all other possible relationships can be excluded.

The rejection of God and the breakdown of relationships mean that community suffers – our leaders even question if such a thing as society exists. The result can be a blind egotism that becomes impervious to injustice. The absence of God, the rejection of values, can mean a world of self-absorbed individuals driven by technology, achieving commercial success but with no feeling for the planet and no sense of a social audit.

It is in this context that people today need to hear John of the Cross's uncompromising message and to ensure that the essence of its content is made accessible to all. It is a teaching with substance. Even if at times John can sound fierce, pessimistic or demanding, what he has to say has a value that gives him every right to challenge his reader. He is a teacher whose message brings freedom, the freedom that allows each human being to realize their self, their person, in its fullness. John of the Cross would echo the gospel saying, 'The truth will set you free' (JOHN 8:32).

The Reality of God

What John wrote had its roots first and foremost in the Scriptures. The Carmelite tradition has always been one of immersing oneself in the Scriptures. Present-day Carmelites have been helped to continue this tradition by members of the Order who are biblical

scholars. Their insights help their fellow Carmelites in their praying the Scriptures. John's theological formation and his studies at
Salamanca offered a solid basis in theology. It is true that he did
not go on to extra years of academic study but his overall formation was sound. Finally, John drew on his own experience of prayer
and the traditions of the Carmelite order. Mention has been made
of works like *The Institutions of the First Monks*, a fourteenth-
century treatise which challenged Carmelites to see union with
God as their *raison d'être*.

The Order's tradition holds that we can all experience the reality of God in this life. A modern Carmelite who expounded that
reality was the Dutchman, Titus Brandsma. Titus, an academic
and a journalist, proclaimed his beliefs in the face of Nazi domination of his homeland, Holland. On his way to the death camp after
his arrest by the Gestapo, his meditations on the cross led to his
own experience of mystical union that enabled him to face physical death in Dachau.

Titus was strongly influenced by John of the Cross and he gave
many courses of lectures on the Saint at Nijmegean University.
Christ's cross – indeed the whole Paschal Mystery – is at the heart
of John's teaching. The Paschal Mystery, for Christians, concerns
the life of Jesus, his suffering, death on the cross and resurrection,
through which God has established a new intimate relationship
with the human race. The first great relationship was established
as the Israelites passed over from slavery to freedom under Moses.
Jesus suffered, died and rose at the time the Passover was being
celebrated, hence he is the new Passover and the event is known
as The Paschal Mystery.

What is at the core of Jesus' saving work is the reality which
reaches its triumphant outcome in the resurrection. The new fullness of life is only achieved by embracing the cross, offering oneself
in loving obedience to the Father, even in death. For John of the
Cross, the Paschal Mystery and its central role in Christian life was
vital. Not for nothing when he entered the Reform did he add 'of

the Cross' to his name. The cross stands for loving trust of the Father. It states that we will allow God freedom in our lives, and that suffering and love lead to the moment when, as in *The Living Flame*, we encounter God's Holy Spirit, the personification of divine love. It will lead to the possibility of union with God in this life and resurrection after physical death.

The diagram of the Mount of Perfection which John made for the nuns at Beas showed that following the narrow path of the gospel we can journey to the place where God's glory dwells. However, if we want to attain union with the One who is everything we have to travel by the way of *nada*, that way of detachment which brings true freedom. God is the one who lovingly invites us into this union and our response given in unquestioning generosity is the way of *nada*, allowing God freedom.

It is at this point that many commentators have found John austere, even objectionable. He has been called a fakir, and Abbot Chapman, an English Benedictine, thought of him as a Buddhist. It is easy to see his use of *nada* (nothing) as a way of escaping from the material world into a world of the mind, a world of rigorous self-discipline. Here we have a paradox, because John loved nature and obviously loved a whole variety of people – his relatives, his brother friars, the nuns and people who were special to him like Doña Ana and Teresa of Avila. He loved walking, feeling the sun and the wind on his face, and his poems show how the Spanish countryside with its wild beauty touched his heart. He loved gardening, he appreciated the very texture of stone used in building new priories, and to put a stop to outbreaks of seriousness and false austerities among the friars he would organize impromptu picnics and shake the over-zealous out of their self-importance. John could be strict on himself because he knew himself and knew his own limits. However, when it came to his confrères, he would advise them to live the rule of the Order and if they decided to live a more austere way, to remember the call to moderation which is at the heart of the Rule. Austerity, asceticism for its own sake, could end up as an ego trip.

John did not ask that those he was guiding should turn their back on life. What he was saying was that God is everything; nature and people in themselves, are as nothing. The way to come to love people and value our planet is to see them as God sees them in a loving, sustaining gaze. John does not want people to lose their identity, because after all it is the unique person that God loves and is calling into the relationship. What John is against is putting anything before God. He wants everyone to be free so that they can soar on eagles' wings, as even a silken thread can hold an eagle down. *Nada* is the true freedom that is meant to take us away from all that is negative in our lives and, above all, free us from alienation.

Denial

For us in the twentieth century, it is not just our own personal wrongdoings which prevent us putting God at the centre of our lives. It is the way society is structured. The way it operates with its presuppositions and at times its blindness. The market economy and the freedom that is supposed to follow in its train is great for some but brings suffering to many others. Certain things become essential and dominate lives. The motor car is a symbol of independence and freedom, yet it can be at the cost of ruining the atmosphere and at the expense of public transport.

Besides such obvious idols there are also the shadows and burdens of human inheritance. Over fifty years on, the world has yet fully to come to terms with the events of the Second World War. Few have been willing to acknowledge the crimes that both sides committed. We remember Nazi or Japanese atrocities, but talk of Dresden or Hiroshima is still regarded as unpatriotic. The shadow of the past still encourages violence in Northern Ireland and elsewhere, with people's fears fuelled by leaders who glory in violence. The West, through NATO and the UN, cannot always be honest. Nowadays, when we kill civilians in military operations we hide behind phrases such as 'collateral damage' – we cannot face facts and say a hospital was bombed by mistake.

John in his age knew of comparable denials. The cruelty of the Conquistadors in the Americas, the social inequality of which he had been a victim, and the imposition of orthodoxy by the Inquisition. John would want all of us, whether sixteenth-century nuns or twentieth-century folk, to be free from idols and totally open to God.

For John, *nada* was a God-given value, enabling us to see how everything speaks of the glory of God. Time and again in his poetry, Gerald Manley Hopkins (1844–1889) speaks of the glory of God in creation. 'The world is charged with the grandeur of God,' he proclaims in 'God's Grandeur'. This is no romantic cry but rather the prayer of a poet who could see the vision of creation. James Joyce (1882–1941), who felt that there was an essential conflict between poet and priest, often spoke of 'Epiphanies'. These were moments of sudden beauty, like the sheen of the sun on a wet slate roof, a sudden unexpected beauty which surely John of the Cross would have loved.

Ross Collings, an Australian Carmelite, in a recent study on John of the Cross reminds his readers that if they have a good theology of creation they can better understand how, for John, *nada*, the way of renunciation, does not clash with his joy in created beauty. Creation is not something in the past, nor is redemption, the process of God's saving work. They are both a process going on all the time with the love of God wanting to touch our world.

John reminds us of something basic to human experience, that two contraries cannot coexist. We have to give ourselves to God's sovereignty because if we give our hearts to the limited we will be limited. The heart has to be free to grow in God's love. As Jack Welch, an American Carmelite, says: 'We were made for great loves, little loves diminish us.' John is asking that in faith we surrender ourselves to the mystery that is God. God wants right relationships with us and we need to have a singleness of purpose and a clear vision so that we can attain the summit of the Mount of Perfection. John prefers, in his way of *nada*, the difficult to the easy, and he sees life that costs as the way to bring out our true humanity. In all of this we do not lose our identity but gain freedom from slavery. Also, if we discover our true identity through closeness to God then we can begin to value people more profoundly and our relationships will be based on an awareness of human dignity that flows from our being like to God. We are, as St Paul says, 'God's work of art' (EPHESIANS 2:10).

The Way of the Night

The way of *nada* is the way of the night, the way of faith. The word 'night' is perhaps one of the most powerful in John's teaching and yet it can be off-putting. The night is not a denial of life, but rather through the night we seek a way that will lead to union with God, the Beloved. This is a union that can best be described as a Mystical Marriage. Night stands as a symbol for purification, for escape from all that is negative, and it is also a place where true light is encountered. Again, to understand what is really meant by night in John's writing then the reader must see what is implied by faith.

Faith, for John, was part of our deepest self that is willing to accept truths revealed by God, truths that transcend natural light and exceed human understanding. In a multi-faith society, the question can be asked, Whose revelation do we accept? This book is based in the Judaeo-Christian tradition, the tradition that also formed John. However, that in no way means that other traditions are to be dismissed. John believed that faith was a gift by which God allows us to go beyond reason into the reality of the divine, and that gift is received through praying the Scriptures and living in the community of the Church. Faith is a personal, loving relationship with God, and becomes the bond that links us to other believers. While it is beyond reason, faith, through theology, can be articulated in a coherent manner. But because it does go beyond reason, faith is like a light that is brighter than anything we know.

The way into the experience of the night is the way of *nada*. While John talks about the night under a fourfold division, everyone experiences the night in their own personal, special way. The night can be seen as a path we join as we journey to God, a path which could take us all our middle life. As Dante wrote in *The Divine Comedy*, 'In the middle of life I found myself in a Dark Wood'. For Dante, the end of his journey was at the core of Paradise.

The night can also be likened to *kenosis* – the self-emptying of God in Jesus. When God sent his Son into the world he was willing to empty himself of all that was special and lived as we do, entering into the world of faith, travelling through the night of misunderstanding. Eventually he came to the ultimate night, the darkness of the cross, where his obedience brought him to the deepest sense of desolation, when he felt abandoned and cried out: 'My God, my God, why have you forsaken me?'

John's teaching on the dark night is found in *The Ascent of Mount Carmel* and *The Dark Night*. His inspiration for writing these commentaries had been the way he saw so many people who were supposed to be wise guides being far from helpful, not recognizing where people were at nor giving them the necessary challenges.

The most straightforward part of the journey is the active night of the sense. This involves facing up to ourselves and, because we want God to be the focus of our lives, becoming open to change. This is not a question of personal will-power, rather it is a willingness to recognize what has to change so we can grow as a person. We need, as *The Book of Common Prayer* expresses it, to be willing to acknowledge 'the devices and desires' of our heart. These 'devices and desires' can include all the games people play, ranging from power games to procrastination, or the way we misuse sexuality. Another aspect of facing up to ourselves is acknowledging our feelings, seeing what they are telling us and using them positively. It is well-nigh impossible to grow as a person if we allow our feelings of anger, jealousy or whatever to tick away inside us like a time bomb. Facing up to our feelings and taking appropriate action is a positive way to change and to grow as a person.

The active night of the sense also involves being honest about relationships. Positive relationships are good, but so often we can be possessive or destructive in our treatment of people. A true respect for human dignity will ensure that people are not used and abused. Even more negative is the way people can be idolized so that they feel trapped. The person who has put them on a pedestal is really signifying their own immaturity, as that sort of relationship diminishes both parties.

If a person is willing to be realistic and to allow growth, it is also necessary to face up to one's shadow side. John of the Cross would not have known of this technical term (one which features prominently in the psychology of Carl Jung), but he would recognize the concept easily. All during our life we have pushed underground aspects of reality either because we were told to keep quiet or our super ego was conditioned to behave in certain ways. Often this was to please people, to be correct, to be seen in a good light. We perform, live the roles but can never feel comfortable or really at ease. Anger, frustration and longings simmer away and we can pass a lifetime like this. Brave faces and bleeding hearts! Part of the resolve of the passive night of the senses would be, with the help of wise guidance, a willingness to face up to this baggage, this shadow side. It often means letting go of conventions, it can lead to confrontations but it does mean a healthier and more honest approach to life.

The active night of the spirit is again an area where the individual is involved in making choices that open us up to a more authentic union with God. John is conscious that people can relate more to a concept or an image of God than the very person. He is asking those who have experienced conversion, who have been drawn to God, to take steps to deepen and mature their faith. I believe in our own day John has an important message to those who have experienced a conversion and perhaps are living on a spiritual high. This can be seen in many groups but especially those of a Pentecostal or Charismatic nature. Such groups are found in all the mainstream churches and often in independent churches. At the point of conversion and for an indefinite period afterwards it is possible to feel great satisfaction in the new relationship with God. The fellowship of the group is vital and certain ways of praying and worshipping take on great importance. It then becomes possible to go to services, to engage in devotions because they are satisfying and become an end in themselves. For Catholics, there is also the bias towards visions – apparitions and certain places can be invested with immense importance. Also, ways of prayer become 'canonized', and the day is incomplete without having said this or that prayer.

John does not see this type of prayer life as deepening faith or bringing a person out of themselves so that they can be touched by the flame of the Spirit's love. What he proposes at this stage is a willingness to give up reliance on what the individual does and begin to practise contemplative prayer, which consists of a trusting waiting on God. John would also want us to move towards a reflective reading of Scripture. And in all this there should be a willingness to be still before the mystery of God. John, in stressing the Scriptures and inner peace, was going back to his Carmelite roots and to the traditions of prayer that had come down through the Middle Ages, such as *Lectio Divina*, the practice of quiet, reflective reading of the Scriptures. It is likely that he would have known of the exercises of St Ignatius as he had attended a college directed by the Jesuits, and by 1580 Ignatius' methods would have been widely diffused. John, however, would have seen the exercises as a step towards contemplative prayer, vital for beginners, but too systematic for the vision he had of a deeper immersion into the mystery of God.

John's attitude to a great deal of piety was firm. While he would have understood the value of popular religion, he was against the one-upmanship that went with running after the latest vision, miracle or whatever. He had nothing against people having a favourite image or finding a certain place helpful for prayer but all these things were in the end relative.

The passive night of the spirit and sense can seem daunting, and I believe it is important to see the end they are meant to achieve. This purification is a gift from God and enables us to reach a close-ness to God that is beautiful and beyond our human conception. This stage in a person's growth is therefore, like anything to do with faith, a gift. It is a time of longing for God, filled with a sense of absence. It calls to mind the words of the Psalm:

As a deer longs for flowing streams,
so my soul longs for you, O God. (PSALM 42:1)

John's experience of the night occurred during his imprisonment and when he came close to God in an amazing union. So John is not retailing some system but making sense of his own life and hoping that what he has to say will benefit others. Also, it must be noted that each of us will make our own journey according to our unique being.

The passive night affects the whole of the person, and John asks that we trust in what is happening so that God can be God for us. The way into this period is a time when prayer becomes almost impossible. It can feel that God is abandoning us and the pain of feeling you have lost the Beloved becomes almost unbearable. Peace and joy depart and are replaced by depression and loss of self-esteem. As in any state of loss, we can feel bewildered and wonder just what has gone wrong. This is the time when we are being asked to share with Christ in a death by which we say yes to God in an unconditional way. In the dark there is a light, but as yet we are unable to grasp what is beyond our comprehension. John is, as it were, displacing death and its fear from its usual biological moment to a place in the life of faith. He is reminding us of the theme of John's gospel, that to believe in Christ is to have eternal life. The act of belief for John is radical, the consequence is to taste now the beauty of the fullness of life.

What is interesting about John's experience of night is that it occurred when he was being persecuted, misunderstood. He became powerless on every level. John was imprisoned because in the midst of an all too human tangle, his goodness became threatening. John was in fact trying in all simplicity to live an ideal, he was wanting to be prophetic and faithful to the gospel. His predicament reminds us of so many great figures in Christianity who have suffered for their love of God either through persecution or being misunderstood. Titus Brandsma and Edith Stein, both Carmelites, were people of faith who were overwhelmed by the darkness of the Nazi ideology and yet through the cross they achieved a marvellous union with God. But what about the many others who have suffered at the hands of the Church because their message was not understood, because they were pioneers. In our own century, figures like Yves Congar and Bernard Häring spring to mind. Again, the diaries of Anne Frank and many of the Beirut hostages show journeys akin to the dark night. In particular, Brian Keenan's book *An Evil Cradling* tells a story that John would have understood.

The night, then, is a time of powerlessness and with a sense of the gulf between oneself and God's holiness. The feeling of isolation and of seeming failure makes the figure of Job seem an apt comparison. How could anyone love this wretchedness and failure?

John, however, would not want us to see this process as some terrible ascetic ordeal. One thing must be clear – the passive night is God's action and the key is to trust and wait and believe in the dawn. We live in the hope that God will possess us.

The way of *nada* has then been well-trodden through the experience of the night. The journey has been freely entered upon and the motive for the journey has been love. We know that nothing can take the place of God in satisfying our needs and the night has shown the deep caverns of our being that only love can fill. And the experience of the night has been the end of false gods. We recognize the aching and longing which only God can satisfy.

Close to God

The purpose of the journey has been love, and the Lover in 'The Dark Night' and the 'Canticle' can go out in full freedom to find the Beloved. The search is possible, union can take place. Love is the God-given energy and that love is the Spirit's gift. But it is also a purifying flame which takes away any obstacle to union with the Beloved – we can now be close to God. Love makes us like God as sin is destroyed, and that same love has given us the trust to journey open to God's ways, even when the whole affair has felt like utter risk.

Obviously, the joy of coming into a close relationship with God is something that few people can articulate. John's poems have done that through powerful symbols and because he was able to find words that even surprised him by their power. However, what stands out in John's writings is the language he uses about our union with God. It is the language and images of the most tender and fulfilled human loving. This is powerful news for our own times because it tells us that human love at its most sublime is the best image we can find for how God and ourselves can relate. It also raises the question of whether we need some experience of human tenderness to begin us on the journey to God. I believe that how we love each other and how we love God is reciprocal, the one affecting and enhancing the other. The journey into God which John shows us is a journey where possessiveness goes and faith, trust and love find freedom to flourish. It is because true human growth and freedom is realized that we can come close to God. If growth and maturity has occurred in our innermost being, then we are able to take up our human relationships in a mode that is gentler, deeper and more understanding of the other.

John's life was one that gave space and time to love and friendship. He felt a freedom in intimacy, he neither wanted to possess nor be possessed. He could celebrate friendship and was honest in the joy such relations brought him. The mystics, because they are open to the loving wisdom of God and allow the love of the Spirit freedom, achieve a humanity that is creative, sensitive and spontaneous. Perhaps one of the great contributions of teachers such as John of the Cross for today could be that in enabling people to grow in loving trust of God and experience unconditional love, men and women would gain confidence in the possibility of achieving a fully loving relationship. Mysticism could well be a school for marriage!

There has never been more talk about relationships and yet there has never been greater difficulty it would seem in living them out. It appears we do not know what we want from each other and the hurt and the anger all this causes is terrible. Can John's *nada* lead to a *todo* for people wanting to find love and deep relationships? I believe it can, because John will help us discover the other in all their beauty and he has so much to say to the devices and desires of our hearts.

$$(\,5\,)$$

John and Spiritual Direction

John of the Cross was concerned that people seeking union with God had good guides or spiritual directors on their journey. He was aware of the harm that unwise, bad advice could have on a person. People seeking God, trusting another in the most intimate longings of their beings, need genuine guides. John's concern is perhaps even more valid today when we see the damage that can be done by enthusiasts, charlatans and so-called guides who in the end can abuse the power and trust afforded to them.

In writing about John as a spiritual director I must acknowledge a debt to the work of two North American Carmelites, Kevin Culligan and Denis Graviss. Denis Graviss analyses the hallmarks of John's work as a spiritual director, while Kevin Culligan explores the interface between John and modern client-based therapy.

Spiritual direction is perhaps as old as Christianity. People have always sought help in their journey to God from contemporaries that they perceived as having deeper experience. It is a ministry of one Christian to another so that they can journey well. Over the years, Carmelites have been sought out as guides in matters of the spirit. English medieval Carmelites were directors to people such as Margery Kempe.

John was concerned that those who helped people towards union with God should be qualified and sensitive. John saw a good director as an exceptional person because, as he observed in *The Living Flame of Love*, 'They must be more than wise and discreet, they have to be experienced'.

John, however, believed that the first and best guide was always God. He often talks of God's guidance using or naming the ways the various persons of the Trinity act in us. Jesus teaches us by example, the Holy Spirit brings wisdom into our lives, while God the Father draws us to a substantial union. The key way in which God helps us is by allowing his wisdom and love to take over in our lives and liberate us from negative feelings and desires. However, John understands that we often need help from another human being to make sense of what is going on in our lives. It is all too easy for us to misinterpret the reality of what God is doing in the core of our being.

The spiritual director has a crucial role which requires immense sensitivity, since he or she is concerned with the complete experience of the person they guide. The director has to be sensitive to the person and able to discern the meaning of God's action in the person's life. John realizes that the director's work has many facets – teaching, parenting, guiding. A guide who supports is perhaps the best shorthand for what is entailed in this work. This means the director has to have an excellent interpersonal relationship with the client, one of respect and awareness of the uniqueness of that person. John sees Jesus as the role model – our brother, our companion on the way. Jesus always listened and would ensure that in every sense he was alongside the person with whom he was involved. A director is a brother or sister, a soul friend. For John, ordination was not a prerequisite for this work; any man or woman with the right qualities could be a spiritual director. The qualities are experience, wisdom and discretion.

Experience means that a person has lived life in a full sense. Nobody can communicate what they have never experienced. The director should be someone who has come close to God in love and also has deep love for people. Experience breeds sensitivity and a way of understanding that can best be described as intuition. Sensitivity means drawing out the other person's gifts and not imposing one's own opinions. A good director leaves room for the Holy

Spirit and is not possessive. When a client may need help from someone other than the director, they should be free to do so.

Wisdom, for John, was a gift of the Holy Spirit. Wisdom came not from some intellectual process but it was special knowledge of God, a way of loving. It also involves having that sort of imagination which prevents us missing what is really going on in a person's life. Wise directors are always reflecting back to their own relationship with God so that they can act as creative channels for God's love to be transmitted into another person's life.

The third quality John looked for was discretion. Discretion was linked to prudence. It meant that the individual and the individual situation were given their proper value. Clear thinking is required when assessing a person's motivation. If necessary, it could mean that mistaken motivation had to be highlighted and corrected.

The wise, prudent, experienced director makes sure that boundaries are set and respected in the relationship. These boundaries are important as they prevent misunderstanding and any hint of the relationship being abusive. What matters is that room is left for Christ and Christ always remains the goal and the model.

Contemporary Psychology

John, writing in the sixteenth century, worked out of a psychology linked to medieval theology. John refers to our faculties the will, the intellect, the memory, whereas modern psychology is based on perception. Is John's approach foreign to how we deal with people today, or can bridges be built? Kevin Culligan sees the possibility of modern therapeutic psychology casting new light on John's work of spiritual direction. He sees behavioural science adding insights to established practice in spiritual direction.

The question is, How can a synthesis be made between John's teaching and the work of contemporary psychology? In his writings, Culligan cites the work of Carl Rogers, which is client-centred, as a possible point of contact. Rogers, like John of the

Cross, proposes definite criteria which should underpin the work of a therapist. The therapist should be genuine, caring and understanding towards the client. For Rogers, the aim of his work was to enable whoever he worked with to become a fully functioning person. Along the way to that goal, he saw the need to help his client find a unity between experience of life and their concept of self — the need to bridge the gap between reality and how I perceive reality. He also explores how the potential within us for realizing our self can be tapped and developed. The therapist helps create conditions for growth through care and understanding and by the commitment to being genuine.

If we look at John's teaching, he would stress that God working in us through the ordinary processes of our humanity helps us towards union with God and the attainment of peace. John, like Rogers, has a goal, and his insistence on criteria such as discretion are not unlike Rogers' criteria. A director should care and should, by their understanding, enable the client to realize their potential.

Rogers, when insisting on congruence between the self and experience, is asking for realism. John states that our well-being flows from the quality of our conscious relationship with God. Our being can flourish if it is grounded in the reality of God and not some image we have created. Again, often a spiritual director has to point out to a person that they are not quite so advanced in their journey, that there is a lack of congruence between where they are and their perception of themselves. It is easy to be deluded about holiness.

The caring and understanding of the director then enables the real work of change which will help towards genuine closeness to God and appropriate behaviour to begin. The quality of the relationship between director and client is crucial. The director does not impose anything but creates a climate where the client begins to recognize the shortcomings in their life.

The notion of 'congruence' found in modern therapy corresponds to a sense of realism in our relationship with God. Our models of holiness have to bear some relationship to our experience, otherwise we can be into dysfunction, displacement activity and denial. A married person cannot act like a monk, nor do external practices guarantee inner growth. In this context, being counselled towards self-denial is not something exotic but rather a call to greater realism. This is also being genuine – to face up to truth about ourselves.

Caring, by which a client is accepted as a unique person and valued for what they are, ensures that the person is respected. This respect is not unlike the New Testament *agape*, a non-possessive yet deep love for the person as they are. Understanding – in the sense of experiencing the other person's inner world 'as if' it were our own – is yet another aspect of non-possessive love. The result of such an attitude is the growth of a trusting relationship which can become a model for other relationships. In spiritual direction, the sense of love and trust generated in this process helps people believe they can be loved by God. The more a person feels helped the more they can believe they can relate to God. Feelings of unworthiness and inadequacy can be left behind.

Experience

Both John and modern therapy value experience. For John, everything has a validity in helping us journey towards God, while Carl Rogers would see the here and now as the seed-ground of values – the building blocks for personal fulfilment. For Rogers, as we develop we should become more open to experience and, as a result, more trusting and creative.

John would see us moving away from negative desires and letting go so that the full reality of God can break out in our lives. Rogers values the energies that let us move from rigidity into a deeper sense of freedom. For John, the journey to God in love helps us become a real person, as we let go of religious conventions. John saw rigidity and misplaced piety as obstacles to union with God.

He would agree with modern therapy that rigidity is a barrier on the way to being the person God wants us to be. Spiritual direction leads us to a genuine relationship with God, and this must include a greater knowledge of ourselves. Prayer and therapy can both claim to bring us to greater self-knowledge. We see ourselves as we are. Prayer helps us see ourselves gaining our worth from our relationship with God and knowing we have deep worth helps us respect and value others as that is how they are in their turn before God. Self-awareness and a coherent sense of our own worth are crucial, and both come from having a goal realized objectively, and this can happen both in therapy and in the way of the mystic. The two are not in opposition, nor are they liable to contradiction.

Over the years, John developed a great capacity for observing where people were at in their search for God and in trying to find overall meaning in life. His deep, genuine love for the people he was guiding meant that he grew more and more sensitive in understanding the process by which they tried to grow. His ability to be so empathetic – so willing to be caring and understanding – created a wonderful climate of trust. It was through that warmth of approach that those helped by John felt able to explore their inner selves and so grow and develop. People are often very shy, diffident and uncertain in talking about what is going on in their inner lives. John because he cared, allowed people to express their feelings and he was then from his own experience able to guide such people with genuine understanding and respect. Also, John would be enriched as he was allowed to observe God's working in that person's life. Being a companion to a person on their inner journey is a privilege, allowing others to see the variety and beauty of people's experience of God. Often the sharing between a spiritual director and their client can produce insights that have a validity for the world at large. The understanding of the reality of God can be enriched by these encounters and have greater meaning than abstract theological studies. The translation of such experiences needs the language of imagination.

If the director works creatively with the person being directed, there is deep respect and the danger of misuse of power in the relationship is never in question. Genuine caring and discreet work will never descend into manipulation or the imposition of the views or opinions of the one who could claim to be more experienced. This point needs to be emphasized, because all too often we read of religious leaders or teachers who use power over people and direct their inner lives in ways that are destructive and can even end in death. John of the Cross offers a way of guidance which has a perennial wisdom, based on a deep respect for the person being guided. For John, the spiritual director and client are companions on the journey, and the treasure, the relationship with God, cannot be compromised by anything that comes in the way of God's work.

Modern therapy emphasizes the need for quality in our interpersonal relationship at whatever level of life. Where good relations exist, whether at work, in the home, in education or in the Church, then growth and positive change take place. We can let go and move if we feel trust in the environment in which we operate. Where relationships are lacking in quality and depth, then we have problems – life goes askew and, so often, inappropriate or dysfunctional behaviour flourishes. Spiritual direction is an interpersonal relationship, and, if we focus on John of the Cross, we see he is a reliable guide because he is so concerned to be caring and understanding with the people he helps.

John, through his wisdom and experience, worked to respect the individual and create the atmosphere where the person is at ease. This is a far cry from any system being imposed or the individual being used or abused by some guru. No, once a person feels recognized for who they are, they feel at ease and the world of their spirit can be explored. Spiritual direction in this sense, as it discovers the world of the human spirit, takes us beyond the senses, showing us that there are realities in the human person that go beyond our normal perceptions of time and space. They are not quantifiable in scientific terms, but they are real because they represent what goes on in the core of our being. Behavioural experts like Rogers admit this possibility, and the work of spiritual directors inspired by John of the Cross give us insights into the mind, body and soul relationship which are crucial.

John and those who continue his work in spiritual direction take us into the mystery of God. Whenever there is talk about attempting to understand God we are always brought back to our attempts at understanding the human person and how that person can relate to God. It is this specialized work of exploration that is the particular remit of spiritual direction. Such work takes us towards the transcendent, what John might call the 'secret'. The spiritual director in the twentieth century who is in dialogue with those who work with client-based therapy will want to talk to the world of behavioural science and ask that world to take note of his findings. Because the spiritual director is moving into areas of experience which do not fit easily within received categories, is this research to be dismissed, or is it to be seen as a new field for the behavioural scientist to examine? It has always been held by Christian thinkers that there is only one truth. Spiritual direction, client-based therapy and other disciplines can help in developing our understanding of what it is to be human, and also the possibility of being open to the transcendent.

Suggested Further Reading

John's Own Works

The Collected Works of St John of the Cross, translated by Kieran
Kavanaugh, OCD, and Otilio Rodriguez, OCD, ICS Publications,
1991.

The Dark Night of the Soul and The Living Flame of Love, Fount
Paperbacks, 1995.

St John of the Cross Poems, with a translation by Roy Campbell,
Penguin, 1960.

Other Works

Brenan, Gerald, *St John of the Cross his life and poetry,* Cambridge
University Press, 1973.

Collings, Ross, OCD, *John of the Cross,* Liturgical Press, 1990.

Culligan, Kevin, OCD, *A Comparative Study of John of the Cross &
Carl Rogers,* Carmelite Studies 2, ICS Publications, 1982.

Graviss, Denis, O Carm, *Portrait of the Spiritual Director in St John
of the Cross,* Institutum Carmelitanum, 1983.

Johnston, William, *Mystical Theology,* HarperCollins, 1995.

Matthews, Iain, OCD, *The Impact of God,* Hodder and Stoughton,
London, 1995.

Murphy, Roland E., O Carm, *The Song of Songs,* Augsburg Fortress,
1990.

Welch, John, O Carm, *When Gods Die,* Paulist Press, 1990.

Index